The Road Ahead and Miles Behind

THE ROAD AHEAD AND MILES BEHIND

A STORY OF HEALING
AND REDEMPTION
BETWEEN FATHER AND SON

MIKE LIGUORI

NEW YORK

LONDON • NASHVILLE • MELBOURNE • VANCOUVER

THE ROAD AHEAD AND MILES BEHIND

A Story of Healing and Redemption Between Father and Son

Published in New York, New York, by Morgan James Publishing. Morgan James is a trademark of Morgan James, LLC. www.MorganJamesPublishing.com

Proudly distributed by Ingram Publisher Services.

Morgan James
BOGO™

A **FREE** ebook edition is available for you
or a friend with the purchase of this print book.

CLEARLY SIGN YOUR NAME ABOVE

Instructions to claim your free ebook edition:
1. Visit MorganJamesBOGO.com
2. Sign your name CLEARLY in the space above
3. Complete the form and submit a photo
   of this entire page
4. You or your friend can download the ebook
   to your preferred device

ISBN 9781631958151 paperback
ISBN 9781631958168 ebook
Library of Congress Control Number:
2021949473

Cover Design by:
Christopher Kirk
www.GFSstudio.com

and Jerry Lazaro

Interior Design by:
Chris Treccani
www.3dogcreative.net

PG | PARENTAL GUIDANCE SUGGESTED
SOME MATERIAL MAY NOT BE SUITABLE FOR CHILDREN

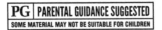

Morgan James is a proud partner of Habitat for Humanity Peninsula and Greater Williamsburg. Partners in building since 2006.

Get involved today! Visit MorganJamesPublishing.com/giving-back

For my dad, who gave me the memory I always wanted.

TABLE OF CONTENTS

ACKNOWLEDGMENTS

There were many people who helped me write this book and have fueled my dream to tell stories to the world. Before I mention the list of people, there is one person who gave me the hope and inspiration to believe in myself: Professor Turner. You have done more for me as a writer and friend than you will ever know. Thank you for being an amazing teacher and helping me find my voice in the world.

To my mom, for never letting me give up on my dream, for telling me I should have been a writer my sophomore year of high school. For being my biggest cheerleader, advocate, and fan; I am truly blessed to have you as my mother.

To my editors, Jillian Buckley and Cortney Donelson, thank you both for shaping and crafting this story to be shared with the world. I could have not done this without your feedback, your time, and your energy.

To my publisher, Morgan James, for believing in this story, believing in me, and helping make this book come to life.

To my brothers and family, thank you for keeping me grounded, for loving me through thick and thin. I am truly blessed to have you in my life.

Finally, to my dear friends. Writing this story was one of the most challenging endeavors of my life. Thank you for your unwavering support and love. Thank you for standing in my corner, for your loyalty, and for doing life with me. I will never forget it.

FOREWORD

Yesterday, I was surprised that my son, Michael, asked me to write this foreword for his new book. It was just the furthest thing from my mind. Well, I know how to write business letters, emails, and that kind of stuff, but to write like "real literature"—man, that's totally new territory. I have always driven a lot. Even as a young man, I would drive sixty miles each way to see my girlfriend. I drove long distances to work too. It is just in my nature. I like to drive, especially a vehicle that has personality. That's how this story starts.

About three years ago, I acquired a Sprinter, a big white cargo van. There was nothing inside it except two seats. Being slightly handy, along with partnering with Kellan, my youngest son, we set out to make this vehicle road-worthy. A second passenger seat, 110-power, and the best thing of all: a refrigerator. At this time, I knew we were going to ride in it, but I wasn't sure where, when, and who would be aboard. I have four sons. Two are in college and two are working their way through life.

It was sometime about two years ago, I had this idea of driving to Florida for the "24 Hours of Rolex" race. I love "big-time" racing. Sports cars are my favorite. So I set out in mid-January, driving Route 40. I stopped to see my son at SMU in Dallas and then drove on for five days, staying in motels and logging 600 to 700 miles a day.

America is a very big place and when you drive along and look at this place, you'll always be amazed at what the early settlers did. Tough is not a good enough word to describe them. Anyway, I digress. After the race, I parked my van in Florida and flew home. I thought it was fun. And *fun* is my motivation,

So time passed and COVID-19 struck, totally disrupting the race season and everything else. Finally, in November 2020, the Sebring 12 Hours race is back on. One day, I reach out to Michael (Mike) and say I have an extra ticket. He says, "I'll go."

I'm a little surprised; Mike is not a big race fan, but I welcomed him as the shotgun. We hadn't really spent much time "*mano y mano*," but I really don't overthink these kinds of things. I just set out to get the trip planned and provisioned.

As with any of the Liguori men, we spent the first twenty-four hours establishing what you're going to tell me and what you're not. So we have our moments of getting short-termed pissed at each other, but then the road takes over. We start to see the drylands of the Southwest, big trucks on the road all going somewhere. Then times where we are the only vehicle in sight. Nothing for miles.

In these spaces, Mike has the true gift of gab. He asks me questions about my childhood, how I viewed him as a kid, and how I got to where I am. How I met his mom . . . questions about each of his brothers. That's when I realized that this trip was so much more than just getting to Sebring. I was passing on my story of how I came to California, how I went through free love in San Francisco, and how I survived some really dumb things I did.

My dad did the same thing. He told me about his life in Hell's Kitchen in New York City, about how rough it was. How you had to keep your eyes open, make sure bad people were not taking advantage of you, etc. You had to protect your family from this stuff.

The trip became about revealing my views of the world and what my experiences had taught me. Now, did I expect him to listen? Not really, but in the realm of the Liguori family story, my story was just part of the mosaic. I realized it was important to pass this stuff on. Plus, we were having fun, laughing at how Mike's Old Man made it out alive time and time again.

Mike then pulls out a microphone and really turns on his *podcast master* hat. I was being interviewed! By my son!

Funny stuff rolls out. Mike fills in his views of me. Some are not the best things a parent wants to hear, but I feel us growing up and open as we motor along. None of this was intended or planned for. It was just happening.

The road trip was the stage, we as the players entered, and the words simply flowed. I learned that Mike is his own man (thank goodness), has seen much, and has a different view of life than me. I learned to respect that. As we drove, the disparity between us narrowed. Mike is half my age, I realized his experiences and views are really very interesting as I filtered them through my own thoughts. Hey, this son of mine is a sharp cookie (as my dad used to say). "Family sayings" are the lore, adding to our group's identity.

As the road unfolded before us, we encountered our good earth expressing itself. Rain, cold, wind, and even a good snowstorm reinforced that we are two men on a journey, and the thoughts poured out of us. Most of the time, we laughed at our stories, our silliness, and just some of the stuff we think about. We talked about our sons/brothers and laughed at their individual ways. Road trips, we even say, "What a good idea!" Nomads have been doing this for hundreds of thousands of years. They probably talked about the same things. It's in our nature to travel, see, hear, and smell the world.

Mike asked me, "What did you learn or feel about the trip?" The big one for me was that I saw my son expressing and living his life passionately. He is happy and grounded in who he is. Seeing him happy makes me very happy. And he knows, as his dad, I've got his back—always.

Mike and I had eleven days of travel together. Do we know each other better? Hell yeah! Am I a better father for that? Hell yeah! Would I do it again? Hell yeah!

The next trip is scheduled for January 2022. I suppose road trips have become our way of bonding. Next up, I have even convinced my wife that we should drive down to Mike's new house in Arizona for Thanksgiving. But no . . . there won't be a book about that one!

Happy road trip to you, the reader!

—James Liguori

INTRODUCTION

I n a couple of weeks, it'll be my thirty-seventh birthday. I didn't use to contemplate time or wonder where it went, but the last couple of birthdays, I have wondered how in the hell I am in my late thirties already! Where did it all go? The time, the events, the memories. It felt like yesterday that I was living in New York City, wandering the streets of the concrete jungle, trying to find myself. I was working downtown by Wall Street, enjoying the hustle of the city—the constant flow of worker bees escaping and then re-entering the revolving doors of skyscrapers. I found myself many times at evening happy hours, staying up nights and weekends as long as I could to meet the sun. And now, I wake up to the crisp morning air of Colorado hitting me in the face as I walk to my local coffee shop to get my morning caffeine. I am dressed in basketball shorts, a hooded sweatshirt, and moccasins lined with faux fur.

And of course, a mask in hand. I'm arguably living in the craziest period of my life, and that includes two tours of duty in Iraq. Months ago, the country shut down due to COVID-19 infiltrating every single city and state. Everyone and their grandmother were holed up in their house or apartment. Families were separated. Zoom calls were a mainstay in our lives. And I was doing everything I could to not lose my sanity.

Things are a little bit better now, this, the month of November 2020. Small businesses have adjusted to protocols. Most, if not all, food places in my neighborhood have adjusted to takeout and delivery as the main drivers of their businesses. My favorite coffee shop is takeout only. I miss sitting at the bar in the beginning hours of the day, chatting with whoever was working behind the counter. I miss bringing my journal with me and penning everything that's going through my mind.

On this particular day, I grab my coffee and sit outside on the bench, watching the early morning strolls of newly adopted dogs sniffing their way through new territory, the owners equipped with doggie bags in hand and gently begging the excited pups not to pull so hard on the leash.

The leaves are starting to turn, a sign that in a few months, the famed Colorado winters will be here.

My phone rings and it's Dad. I think, *what in the world does he want this early in the morning*? I consider ignoring it, calling him later—maybe when I take a break from working. He probably wants to talk about business or football. That'll help pass some time on this day in the neighborhood. Now, before I tell you about the call, I must tell you about Dad and me.

We have a historically rocky relationship that only found some common ground within the last few years. Safe topics were sports and making money. Everything else, we disagreed on. Politics, faith, and nearly every single choice I made in my life. It's pretty common for us to disagree with our parents. Our parents want what's best for us. We want to discover on our own what's best for us. But for Dad, he wanted me to do things his way. It was his world, and I was just living in it.

He didn't have this rockiness with my other brothers. They were motorheads like he was. If a conversation went awry, they could always find stability within IMSA racing, the ongoing debates between the most superior cars (Audi or BMW). That argument still fills the air when the four of us and him get around each other. Of course, I have no opinion. I would be happy with either one of those cars sitting in my parking spot. But to those guys, they could spend the rest of their lives debating and pontificating over the engines, the transmissions, you name it. They even went so far as to insult each other's abilities to drive a car. That also carries over during our get-togethers. All of my brothers and Dad love auto racing. I am the only one that never fell for it. I wanted to. I tried. I went to races with Dad, to events like Daytona and the Indianapolis 500. I even asked him questions. But I couldn't get into it. My brothers often would shake their heads in disbelief whenever I'd mention that I didn't want to go to another race.

Even Dad would bust my balls about it, saying, *How could you be a Liguori man and not like auto racing?*

Over time, Dad and I had learned our safe zones. We stayed there. We talked about God, but we stayed away from Jesus. We had different views about that too. We didn't talk about love or dating. His track record wasn't something to brag about and, well, I found myself replicating his patterns and choices in my relationships. So we stuck with football. We stuck with running an agency. We stuck with the stock market. And it's cordial between us.

But deep down, in the back of my mind, I wish it wasn't like that between us.

He was rigid in his thinking. He never made me feel like he cared about what I had going on in my life. Even living with my ex-girlfriend at the time, he barely took interest in our updates and what we had going on. It was always about him.

=====

The phone keeps ringing. I start to feel guilty about ignoring his call, so I pick up the phone, cup it in one hand and prepare myself for the same crap, different day conversation.

"Hey, Dad," I answer.

"Michael, how are you?"

"Good, just drinking coffee this morning." There is a bit of a pause, an all too familiar experience when I talk to him.

"Great to hear. Hey, listen. I want to ask you something. So I am headed to Sebring. I've told you about Sebring, right?"

"Yeah, you've mentioned it to me before."

"So it's this big race, tons of fans, the cars . . ." And this is where Dad starts to sell me. Dad is good at sales, even though he's always been the money guy in his businesses. I wouldn't even call it selling. He just knows how to pitch something. It's how he made his money in the ad agency business, sitting across from his clients, telling them about brand campaigns, showing them layouts of billboards and bus stop signs he and his team had designed. I've seen him do it so many times that I have become immune to him when he gets into "Don Draper mode."

"I was going to ask your brothers, but then I thought, you and I have never been. And I was thinking maybe you and I could go together this year. We'll drive across the country in the sprinter van, camp out . . . it'll be fun."

My heart skips a beat. *Is he out of his mind?* I think. How does he have the guts to think I want to be in a car with him for eleven days, hitting the road? I thought for sure he would have asked the other boys first, but he didn't. He asked me. Eleven days in a car with him seems like it could completely shatter my relationship with him once and for all. I could see it create inflammation between us and be the stomping ground for more arguments. As a teenager, I poked and prodded him—just to argue, just so I could feel rebellious and different from him. And as a young veteran fresh out of the military, I stood on the grounds of my experience in war to announce that he—and all his conservative radio shows he immerses himself in—were nothing more than armchair quarterbacks with just their opinions on what US foreign policy really should be.

"You have no clue what you're talking about when it comes to foreign policy," I remember saying to him once in a heated argument, during one of the coldest days of the year in California. I was brimming with anger, frustrated that he could even speak about anything related to war or diplomacy without experiencing it. I felt like a crusty, old veteran, passing time at an American Legion bar with a fifty-cent Budweiser in his hand, reminding myself how messed up war is and that nobody has a right to talk about it unless they've been there. I stood on my self-righteous soapbox for years. I spent immense amounts of energy just to fight him, to be different in any way, shape, or form.

I did everything I could to find reasons to dislike him. The more I dug for reasons, the more I started to hate him. Conjuring that up with his habitual tardiness and always finding a reason to go up to Healdsburg instead of letting me hang out with my friends, I struck paydirt when I stopped talking to him.

During that time of silence between us, he didn't exist to me. I even mentioned to my mom that some of her friends' husbands were more father figures to me than Dad. I drank a lot during that time. I figured it would be easy for me to bury my resentment for him.

We ended up reconnecting after some time—agreeing to start over—but it took a long time for us to meet in a place where simply speaking on the phone felt normal.

When he was pitching me on the phone about Sebring, I still experienced these lingering feelings of resentment and doubt. He had constantly let me down when I was growing up, and every time I thought that maybe one day, it wasn't going to be about money or him prioritizing his wants over others. Maybe he would actually get involved in my life. Maybe he would care enough to be in my world for once, to see what I see. But he never did. It was more of the same, and it got worse as we grew older.

I was ready to say no to him about this trip. I was determined to let him down like he had let me down . . . when something came over me. I don't know what it was but it was familiar. I have felt this presence a handful of times in my life, including when I decided not to commit suicide after battling depression and anxiety for years. When I went to Belgium and experienced chocolate and beer at the same time for the first time. When I fell in love in Portugal. It felt supernatural and unexplainable, and it had found its way into the deep recesses of my mind. I could hear Dad still faintly talking in the background as this voice spoke to me.

"Michael, you need to go on this trip with your Dad. It may be the only one you ever get with him."

Those words pierced my soul. It broke every wall I had built. It transcended my anger toward my dad. It blew past my secret about disliking him. I thought we could never have anything together. But that voice told me otherwise. The voice mentioned nothing of him changing or me changing or anything about us becoming best friends. It only told me to go.

And so I said yes.

═══

It's hard not to think I will become Dad at some point. As I grow older, the chances of me becoming a mix of both of my parents increase by the minute. It's why I laugh at those Progressive Insurance commercials about the guy Rick who coaches people how to avoid ending up like their parents. It's not because they are hilarious. It's because those commercials are true. And I carry some inherent resentment that I'll end up like my dad, no matter how much work I put into not being him. I want to be much cooler than him, much more vulnerable and open with my kids. I want to stay up to date with what they are into, which may be a sign that I should be careful what I wish for. I don't want to lose touch with them and live in a cocoon made of my own stuff. And the more I try not to be like Dad, the more I become him.

That's what makes my saying yes to him on the phone so uncomfortable. I already have some of his mannerisms and quirks, and they drive me crazy. At times, I say and explain things to people just as he does. The hand gestures, the pausing before making a point, the facial expressions. I caught myself one time in the mirror making the same face he makes when he argues, and I almost lost my you-know-what. The other day, I was pacing around my apartment in thought, hoping a lightning bolt of inspiration would come down from the sky to help me solve whatever problem I was encountering. A metaphorical bolt of lightning did hit me, but it was not one of inspiration. It was catching myself talking like my dad.

The trip to Florida feels like pitting two bulls against each other, interlocking horns until one falters. We're both stubborn as it is. When he spoke over the phone, he sounded full of conviction, without any doubts that this trip was going to be what I needed. I felt like I was being sold on buying one of those timeshares at a convention— something in Hawaii. It just felt like it was too good to be true. I felt like I was going to regret my decision, or at the minimum, had a feeling that he was going to leave me hanging at the hotel waiting for him to come pick me up in Las Vegas. I even saw how it would play out in my mind. He would cancel at the last minute; he would tell me he's changing his plans and going with one of my other brothers. The sheer thought he would leave me hanging— combined with the years of anger, frustration, sadness, and disappointment—felt terrible. More than anything, though—at least as far as the feelings I could name—I felt vulnerable and afraid that this trip was only going to make me angrier, more reactive toward him. It may put the nail in the coffin between us once and for all.

Yet, deep down, I could only say yes. Even if the yes was filled with regret, it honestly felt like divine intervention. I knew nothing of what would happen on this trip. I didn't know how I would survive him in the van with me for eleven days. I just knew I had to go. I could hear a sigh of relief on his end. A sense of "alright, cool, *we're going to do this*. It's going to be fun." And just like all the other times before, I gave in to the fantasy that my dad, for once, was going to be different this time around.

"Sure, I'll go with you. Sounds like a good time," I said.

"Really? Aw man, that will be great. We're going to have a good time," he said. "Alright, I got to go, son. I'll talk to you soon."

He hung up the phone. And there I was, standing in my living room, my phone clenched in the palm of my now sweaty hand. My ex-girlfriend looked at me from the couch, wondering what I had just committed to.

"Guess I'm going on a road trip with my dad."

The plane ride to Las Vegas, with the engine roaring at 30,000 feet, and the sound reverberating through the cabin provides quite the environment to sit and think about thirty years of daddy issues. Up until 2020, my dad was nothing more than a man who was limited in his ability to be the father I thought he should be. And now, we were headed on a cross-country road trip in the form of a Hail Mary effort that intimated Dad and I still had a chance to salvage whatever was left. Little did we know that this trip would change us forever. The stories you are about to read were written during the trip and the week after. I cried when I wrote them. I laughed my butt off rereading them. I realized while writing this book that someday, my dad would no longer be here on this earth, and these stories may be the most cherished memories I will have of him.

It took a cross-country road trip for me to figure out more about the man I am now, the one my father is, and the one I wish to become.

PRIZE FIGHTER

My childhood consisted of two worlds. One of them was Mondays, Tuesdays, Thursdays, and every other weekend with a single mom who only had a house to her name. It was a world of volatility. There were days when we could buy the clothes we wanted, pay a little extra at the grocery store for better food, and get through the month with ease. Then there were days where Mom would walk into the kitchen as I started my search in the middle shelf for some cookies and tell us that this month was going to be "a little tight"—that we were all going to have to watch what we were spending. Some of those days where mom gave us that fiscal warning turned into weeks, and the weeks, at times, turned into months.

Somehow and someway, though, Mom always managed to put food on the table. She managed to keep the power running at a time when my brother and I were playing Sega Genesis for hours on end and watching cartoons in the afternoon, contributing to what was surely a large monthly utility bill. Yet, the water stayed on. The bill collectors never came to the door. For a woman who didn't have a college education and whose sole priority in life was to raise two boys, Mom always made sure we had what we needed. That resolve came from her days working as a flight attendant for American Airlines during the years before I was born, traveling the world with absolute freedom. She was always taking care of others before herself. From time to time, she tells me stories of her days roaming the aisles, serving water and stale peanuts. She'll share encounters with famous people she had as they flew across the country. One time, she held Ray Charles's hand on a flight because he was nervous due to some turbulence. It was one of the highlights of her career. She told me he was the nicest man, telling her he knew how kind her soul was just by the palm of her hand gripping his.

To this day, I do not know how Mom raised two boys—who were far from well behaved—while working multiple jobs and attending school to finally graduate college with honors. On top of that, she overcame a leukemia diagnosis that put her chances of survival at the time at less than 50 percent. She told my brother and me about her diagnosis when I was sixteen. I believed she had received a death sentence. There were periods of contemplating "the why" in the privacy of my bedroom, tears over "inevitable" death, and a forcible upbringing of now becoming the "man of the house." I thought for sure I would have to grow up much faster than I was ready to. But no matter how tall the chips were stacked against her, she never wavered or quit. She never showed worry or doubt in front of my brother or me. She was like a prize fighter, deep into the tenth round of a twelve-round championship fight. She refused to quit, and if she was going to go down, she was going to go down swinging.

Watching Mom go to her chemotherapy appointments and then come back home, a smile on her face as if she had just enjoyed a few cocktails with girlfriends she hadn't seen in a long time was the type of strength only a mother possesses. A couple of weeks before my high school graduation, her doctors told her she couldn't go because her immune system was too weak. My mom told the doctors that she had been waiting her entire life to see her oldest son graduate from high school and that "I'll be damned if I am going to miss this."

On graduation day, the principal had called my name to receive my diploma, and the moment I shook hands with one hand and grabbed the diploma in the other, my eyes locked with Mom's. Armed with an N95 mask and walker, her five-foot-four frame stood tall and out from the crowd. There she was, waving in all her glory without a care in the world, without any regret that she broke out of the hospital against the doctor's advice.

I made my way to her after the ceremony ended, and she embraced me with half the strength of her usual hugs.

"I'm proud of you, and I love you," she told me.

"I love you too, Mom."

She let go of me and told me she had to get back to the hospital. "Doctor's orders," she said.

Years later, when I worked at the hospital where she was treated, I had an encounter with a doctor on the hospital's oncology unit who recognized my last name.

"Is your mom Lori by chance?" he asked.

"Yes, it is. How did you know my mom?"

"I treated her when she was here. Your mom is one of the toughest patients I've ever had. She never quit or gave up."

My mom beat leukemia about halfway through my enlistment with the Marines. We celebrated when I got out. I remember her giving me the look of someone who knew nothing of quitting and everything about perseverance. She smiled as always. It was representative of my whole world with her. Long periods of not knowing where the next paycheck would come from, the formation of dark clouds and storms embodying the uncertainty of another day with her on earth, followed by brief, shining moments in the sun.

Today, there are more shining moments in the sun than storms with her. I watch my mom in her retirement, the Arizona mornings forming their brilliance in her backyard, her cup filled with freshly-brewed, hot coffee, and our dog Apollo, lying by her side. The golden rays of sunlight peek through the half-opened blinds. She spends the early mornings watching Robin Roberts on *Good Morning America* followed by her beloved San Francisco Giants in the evening. This is the happiest and most calm I have ever seen her—ever. She no longer has to worry about much except about whether I have enough groceries in my kitchen, which spurs an impromptu and sometimes overwhelming delivery of Costco and Trader Joe's goods. She does not fear her death, for she has seen enough of it in her lifetime to know every moment matters. She is enjoying her life as much as she should. That is the prize-fighting spirit in her. The years of sacrificing, grinding, and keeping faith, she made it to the top as a champion and will walk away forever as one.

FRIDAY NIGHT SMACKDOWN

Wednesdays, Fridays, and every other weekend were spent with Dad. Fridays were my favorite days with him. Friday nights were the nights we indulged in large pizzas, IBC root beer, and WWF wrestling on the television. Those nights were filled with the glory days of Hulk Hogan, the Macho Man Randy Savage, and the dynamic duo of Animal and Hawk who formed the incomparable Legion of Doom. There was the Nature Boy Ric Flair's grandiose entrance in sequins and purple velvet and the Ultimate Warrior's emphatic run down the main alley.

Those guys were my childhood heroes. They gave me an escape from the back-and-forth traveling between two houses, equipped with a duffle bag full of clothes and sports gear. They distracted me from inherently thinking that the divorce was somehow my fault. Friday night wrestling took me away from the perils of falling behind in middle school arithmetic and constantly finding my butt in detention. Those Friday nights were not just meant for watching wrestling. They were meant for us to wrestle too. Dad, my brother, and I would move the couches to the furthest corners of the living room and lay a padded blanket on the floor, ready to engage in the art of flying elbows and belching contests as a result of pounding root beer after root beer. A Friday night at the Eagle's Nest, the name of my dad's first bachelor pad post-divorce, was my safe haven. It was my heaven on earth. That was until my dad got a new girlfriend.

The once enduring bouts of wrestling on the living room floor—my dad mimicking Andre the Giant or Yokozuna, which only ended when our giant cravings for slices of large pizzas kicked in—were cut short when she came over. Next came a ban on all aerial moves until my brother and I were able to negotiate a firm guideline that allowed some moves but restricted others. Dinner was no longer sitting around the living room coffee table eating pizza straight from the box. It was now held in the dining room, the four of us gathered around an oak-stained table. Friday nights at the Eagle's Nest no longer had much in common with an Elks Lodge. There was a woman now. And that was a kick to the nuts if there ever was one.

Her belongings soon sprouted around the Eagle's Nest and took root. There were photos of her family on the counter near photos of my dad and my brother. Dust from her easel and pastel chalk, where she spent hours drawing, started to coat the trophies that my brother and I were awarded from soccer. Her white Subaru was parked right next to Dad's Ford Bronco. It wasn't long until Friday night WWF started to lose its luster. Before she came into our lives, Dad was fully immersed in Friday Night Smackdown. He took on whatever character was necessary to feed the hero-villain narrative. He'd lower his voice. He'd pretend to speak to the crowd. But when she appeared, the nights of him being present stopped.

My brother and I schemed ways to get rid of her to take back our Friday nights. We thought about dumping ice cold water on her while she was in the shower, followed by the old-school classic: mirroring and mimicking every action and every word she uttered. There was even one plan where slashing her tires would give her the impression that the nice neighborhood in suburbia was actually filled with carjackers, too dangerous to stay in, and she wouldn't come back to the Eagle's Nest anymore. We hoped that she would find my brother and me so annoying that it forced things to go back to the way they were, the way I thought they should have been. Dad, my brother, and I growing up and taking on life together as men.

But then I realized, even at a young age, that Dad was happy. And she was too. They fit each other well. They wanted the same things. It seemed she was going to be part of our world and our lives for the rest of time. And as we get older, I understood, companionship becomes more important. In fact, companionship makes its way to the top of the list and becomes the only thing we want as we make our way to becoming worm food.

Dad has spoken, at times, about his previous marriages, their relationships, and the times when he was not happy—and neither were his wives at the time. It wasn't until he met my stepmom that he felt a sense of hope, a suggestion that maybe the joy of companionship would no longer elude him. He'd finally found something special with her.

As much as I selfishly wanted us men to live life as a male-only tribe for the rest of our eternity, I wanted my dad and my stepmom to be happy, to be in love, to live life together too. I always knew Friday Night Smackdown wouldn't last forever.

Though, of course, I had hoped it would.

FOR THE LOVE OF THE GAME

Dad and I share a special connection with sports. He took me to hockey games, baseball games, and once in a while, basketball games during the week, bringing me home past my bedtime, even when I stayed at my mom's house. On the way to the games, we would grab Taco Bell in the car, eating as he shifted gears driving his Ford Bronco. It was our special meal that we had together. I'd get double-deckers with beans instead of meat. He would do the same. At the games, Dad was a different dad than the one I interacted with at home. He taught me the rules of baseball and encouraged me to cheer for the San Francisco Giants, Golden State Warriors, and San Jose Sharks. He would give me a play-by-play of what was unfolding before me on the field. He'd make sure I was filled to the brim with ballpark food and that there were plenty of Ricola cough drops for the both of us to have for dessert.

I guess that's why we always talk about sports on the phone, especially football.

Dad and I love college football. We went to the Red River Showdown in 2019 in Dallas, Texas. It felt like old times, the two of us wandering around the Texas State Fair, laughing at the assorted amounts of fried food and big, foam cowboy hats. We sat in a stadium with over 90,000 people, equally divided with one side being crimson red and the other burnt orange. Dad and I sat high in the nosebleeds taking in the sights and sounds of the Cotton Bowl. I saw him smiling with pure joy, the Eyes of Texas playing in the background. He shared with me that year that he was thinking about winding down his involvement in his business, taking his chips off the table while he was ahead. Dad has a knack for expressing his feelings at sporting events with me. Dad would take me to games and tell me ideas he had or vent in frustration that he didn't get to balance his checkbook because he was so busy with work. If he had a grievance with one of his business partners or one of my brothers, he would tell me in the open air of a stadium. It didn't matter who was around him, Dad would let it rip in the confines of AT&T Park and Oracle Arena. I would listen to him, even though I had no clue or backstory about what he was referring to. I felt like a therapist wearing a kid's baseball glove, hoping to catch a foul ball while also providing emotional support. I didn't know what to say. I mean, what could I say? I was still a kid and there was my dad, telling me about checks, money, how a client meeting went down, or how mad he was at my brother for acting out in class. As I grew older, I quickly learned that if I wanted to know anything from Dad, get as close to the truth as possible, I could ask him at a Giants game. And so one afternoon, during the summer before I left for the Marines, I asked Dad about him and my mom.

"Dad, did you cheat on mom?"

He paused, fumbling through his bag of peanuts that he always brought with him into the stadium. He looked down at the concrete in front of him, cracked open a shell, and inserted the peanuts in his mouth before throwing the remnants by his shoe.

"I did and I am not proud of it."

We didn't talk much after he said that to me. I knew he wanted to explain himself, but man was I ticked off. He had already built a track record of flip-flopping on promises, but to admit he cheated on the woman who had busted her butt to raise me the best she could . . . I was so close to slugging him in the mouth. And at the time, I wouldn't have cared if I had gotten taken away in handcuffs. That punch would have been worth it to me.

While sports broke open some nasty conversations between Dad and me and gave him a place to express himself, it also gave us a place to amend our differences to where we could at least be on speaking terms.

Another Giants game we attended while I was in college set the stage for us to speak again after not doing so for far too long. It's hard to pinpoint exactly what led to Dad and I not speaking. I quite honestly cannot recall a single moment in time that triggered me to think "Wow! That's the moment I started to dislike my dad." I think it was just a matter of him promising to show up and then bailing many times at the last minute. There were things I was trying to figure out as a young man: women, shaving, driving a car, or how to get a job. I only learned two out of the four from him. Maybe it was the lack of validation that I was worth anything in his eyes. He very rarely pulled me aside and told me he was proud of me. I mean, I wasn't an all-star student or the most well-behaved in class.

I ended up in detention more often than I accumulated Bs and As on my report card. I got more attention from my negative antics than I did from the positive ones. And for some reason, I thought that was the best way to get him to notice me. Act out and he would play Dad. Not be involved in his business. Not be involved or preoccupied with his BMW that was sitting in his garage. Not listening to the radio. "Then," I thought, "he would hang out with me, coach me in life . . . be involved and present."

While I loved the sports games and having the opportunity to go see some amazing athletes play, it was not my favorite place to spend time with him. That was on the beaches of Half Moon Bay in the wee hours of Saturday morning, playing beach football with him. I carried this yellow and burgundy football underneath my arm, my legs shaking in excitement the closer we got to the beach, all in anticipation of running routes and patterns with him as the quarterback. I would pretend to be Jerry Rice, him Joe Montana, and those hours on the beach were one of the highlights of my youth. Sometimes, we would do a mock game, me versus him, and the first one to three scores wins. He would narrate in the voice of the late Keith Jackson. I can still feel the smile on my face and the energy that flowed through my body and hear the waves crashing against the shore. It was bliss, and I wish Dad and I could live doing that for the rest of our lives. It was the only place I ever felt Dad and I were father and son.

I knew it couldn't always be that way between us. But a kid could dream.

9/12/01

Everything changed for me on September 12, 2001. I found myself in the recruiting office of the United States Marine Corps, answering no to any question that would get me disqualified and saying yes to everything that would get me enlisted. Right after my eighteenth birthday, I signed on the dotted line and told my parents I was going to war. My mom, being the emotional caregiver and protector she is, broke down and cried, speaking of my hypothetical death in a combat zone when I had not even left for boot camp. I assured her the only way any child could assure their parents of such a thing.

"Mom, I'm going to be fine."

My decision to enlist got interesting when I told Dad. We were sitting down at the dinner table, to a concoction of fried rice, steamed vegetables, and cheese-and-bean

31

tacos that had been a staple of Dad's cooking since the divorce between my parents. Dinner was the only time Dad did not have work in front of him or he wasn't preoccupied with something on the news. If you were going to tell him anything, good or bad, this was the time to do it. And right when he was about to sink his teeth into his serving of tacos, I told him I had joined the Marines. I expected some sort of jubilation from him—his oldest son serving in the military, more than likely going off to a foreign land in the name of the Global War on Terror. Instead, what I got was him continuing to chomp down on his taco, a kernel of rice hanging off the side of his lip. He stared at the vegetables in the pot placed in the middle of the table. He chewed like a cow, in a circular motion, his eyes never blinking.

"Really?" he said, eventually. "Son, that is incredible. I am proud of you."

I was too early in my years to have a heart attack but holy crap! I felt like I had one. My dad, the man who crunched numbers, who talked mostly about his business and clients as if they were his own children, told me that he was proud of me. Never had he said that before. Not when I would get a rare B on a test that I didn't study for.

Never when I went on a scoring streak in soccer. Even when he found out I was graduating high school on time (though barely passing)—nothing. The moment he told me he was proud of me, I was sure that we would have a breakthrough. I was sure that the years of resentment I held onto would be washed away. They weren't. He went back to eating his food, asking my brother and me to clean the table when we were finished.

The next few hours that night were spent sitting on the couch watching TV. In silence. Not a word about any of it. I was expecting more. I wanted more. And it was then I realized, as I went to my room to turn in for the night, that my dad may never be capable of giving me more than the occasional "atta boy!" or a semi-emphatic "proud of you." I did not understand how a father whose son was leaving for war could only express a verbal sentiment of pride then return to his nightly routine of Fox News followed by the HISTORY Channel.

Yes, Dad was obsessed with his business, with making money, and with his status in the world. But I was going off to war and thought that would have resonated deeper with him. It didn't and little did I know that the

Marines would end up being the father figure I so desperately wanted . . . and very much needed.

I landed on the yellow footprints of the Marine Corps Recruit Depot in San Diego in the summer of 2002. I quickly learned what was needed to thrive as a young man in the world: the tying of a proper Windsor knot, how to wear a uniform, and the meticulous pruning of Irish pennants. And the proper stance and position when firing an M16 rifle from a distance of 300 meters or more to hit the target. There were countless sessions of instruction of Marine Corps Martial Arts with another young, lost soul looking for his own much-needed father figure. We both felt the energy of being given more than enough attention in going from a boy to a man. There was the daily instruction of core values—the words *honor, courage,* and *commitment* drilled into our heads. With each repetition, I waded into the holy waters of the greatest fighting organization the world has ever known. I became a disciple, an apostle, and a rightful owner of the Eagle Globe and Anchor.

During my deployments to Iraq, my letters were enough to tell my dad what was going on and how the desert was treating me. When we talked on the phone, our calls were short enough to let him know I was still alive.

Both times I came home from the war, my dad embraced me with open arms and hugs that I hadn't felt in my lifetime. He would bring me to the athletic club and tell his buddies that his son, the Marine, was home from the war. They would smile, shake my hand, welcome me home, and thank me for my service. I'd acknowledge them with a firm handshake and a thank you.

I wondered—yet again—if things were going to be different between Dad and me. Maybe going to war would change the dynamic between us for the better, but my aspirations were short-lived when I decided to leave the service. He no longer told his buddies about me in the manner of being an active-duty Marine, fighting the good fight for freedom, and deploying to far-off lands. I was now a veteran, an average citizen starting my four-year escapade into college. No longer was I wearing a military uniform. I was wearing a t-shirt and sweatpants. The ribbons I once wore upon my chest to show off what I achieved in the Marines . . . well, those were buried deep within a seabag stacked high on my mom's garage shelf. Instead, I wore a uniform of depression, of anxiety from PTSD.

I was no longer worth parading around.

A ROLL OF THE DICE

It's November 2020, and I still don't know why I agreed to go with Dad on this road trip. As I sit in my hotel room at the Park MGM, dressed head to toe in a gray sweatsuit, a wad of cash bulging in my left pocket, I have no clue what I was thinking. I speak into my phone to record the nervousness I am feeling, staring at the palm trees painted on the wall in front of me. I speak to how conflicted I've been, and how anxious I feel that Dad will be late, maybe not show up to Las Vegas at all. I think of a conversation I had earlier in the year with a close friend of mine who asked me if I truly liked my dad and whether I really loved him. It was over coffee in the middle of spring. It was the first time anyone had asked me this.

"I do, I mean, I accept who he is, ya know . . ."

"That's not what I am asking you," my friend probed. "Do you like him? Is he someone you want in your life?"

"I mean, who doesn't want their father in their life?"

"Not what I am asking. Do you *like* him?"

I paused and stared at the steam coming from my coffee, the early morning wiping it away the moment it reached above the brim of my cup. Birds chirped, filling the momentary silence. Cars drove by with squeaky brakes. Others with music blaring, the bass bumping. I did my best to sit in the noise, but I couldn't. Thoughts of whether I had been lying to myself about him all these years, about whether some relationship with him was better than none at all infiltrated my mind. I wondered if the years I felt pulled apart by the two worlds, wishing I could sit and live in just one, had caught up to me. Maybe it had. And my friend understood. He had gone through the same thing with his dad. And one day, he started to understand that nothing was going to change between them.

So he decided to accept his dad and have something with him, something that was better than nothing. I had done the same—or so I thought—but the difference between my friend and me was that he wholeheartedly accepted that this was going to be the way it was between them. He didn't hold out for hope that things would be different. Sitting in front of my friend, I felt the hatred of the years of tardiness, the back and forth promises of money to encourage my brother and me to do our chores, and more rise up. I felt the regret of trying to always meet Dad where he was at with no reciprocation bursting at the seams to alleviate his apathy toward me.

And for the first time, I told someone the weight of what I'd been carrying for a long time.

"I don't like him at all. I think he sucks as a dad."

The birds filled the air again. The cars continued to drive by. And I cried in sorrow and anguish. Wow—the guilt that ate at me. The peril. My friend put his arm around me and told me that it was about time I shared how I felt, not just with him but with myself. It is an awful feeling to admit you dislike someone you love. It's even worse when that person is your parent. I wanted to like Dad. I wanted to find a place in my heart for him, to love and accept him for who he was. And something was better than nothing with him, even if that meant partaking in conversations that were nothing but surface level. I spent many years wishing I could change him.

And I think now, in this hotel room, that this may be as good as it gets. I hope that at the very least, I can spend the rest of our days together living on cordial ground. I would have something to remember him by, something to say at his funeral someday. It's better than having nothing to say at all.

I had a dream in the months before this trip where I'm standing at the podium at my dad's funeral. Friends of his sit in the back row, in their old age, dressed "to the nines" in suits with matching pocket squares and little jewelry on their hands and wrists. Some of these faces I do not know; others I have seen from time to time. Further up, there are my friends, staring at me, nodding in acknowledgment of their condolences. My mom is there, somewhere in the front row, to pay her respects. She knows more than anyone that finding anything worth saying about Dad is a battle. It is intimidating when the pastor calls my name to give the eulogy of my Dad. I step to the mic and when I speak, nothing comes out. It feels like I have lost my voice. I try to collect myself as I stand there, holding a piece of paper where I had jotted down some notes. Again, when I try to speak, there are no words that come out. I try to find something honorable, something I can pull that shows all-in-all how good of a person my dad was. But I choke on the very thought. In a final attempt to share with the audience the memories of my dad, I am only able to utter the words:

"I have nothing to say."

That dream woke me up in the middle of the night and made my heart race on more than one occasion. I know sharing something meaningful with him for the rest of our days would be better than nothing at all. Even if that means being on the road with him for eleven days, only staying in the arenas he is comfortable speaking and existing in. It would give me something to say when the inevitable day comes, and he is no longer here.

I start to scroll through return flights on my phone, just in case he decides not to come at all. I think I've made a mistake, that I am about to be left behind. He isn't going to show up. Then, I look at my phone and see he's called me twice. There is a voicemail. He tells me that he's in Orange County and should be here soon.

SATURDAYS ARE FOR THE BOYS

D ad rolls up to Las Vegas, windows down, sprinter van lightly coated in dust and bird poop, ready to go. He smiles at me with a relaxed salute from the brim of his IMSA racing ball cap as I approach the van. Stepping down from his captain's chair, he embraces my hand with a firm handshake. It is a handshake I know more than his hugs. Dad taught me the art of the handshake—a firm grip but not too firm as to break someone's hand. A stare into the eyes but not too deep, otherwise the other person will think you're in love with them. Just enough of a stare that the person knows that meeting them is important.

He shakes my hand when he sees me the same way that he taught me. There are split seconds of presentness I get from him before he goes back into his own world, his reality. We catch up on the walk to the hotel room, the first topic being the current state of political affairs, something I had hoped to avoid. We talk about my brothers and how every single one of us is walking our own path. There is a sense of pride beaming from his voice when he talks about us.

"The fact that none of you ended up in jail, homeless, addicted to drugs, or unmotivated about doing something with your lives," he says, "is a straight miracle from God." Dad likes talking miracles. He labels the things he cannot explain or comprehend as such: the mountain ranges of Colorado, a beautiful woman who takes your breath away, the perfect symmetry hidden, yet prominent, in Mother Nature. Those are miracles to my Dad. I don't believe so much in miracles like he does. There are things that have happened in my life that I cannot comprehend or explain, but I don't label them as miracles. Things like coming home from two tours of duty in Iraq, a week in Europe alone traveling to find God in the most unthinkable places, and finding out that I had failed Finance the day I was supposed to graduate college, and my mom not losing her mind with me as she had done when I failed classes in the past. In my eyes, that last one was divine intervention because it took the force of God to keep my mom at such a calm level, not wanting to throw a shoe at me.

All those other events, I don't know what I would label them as. What I know is that they all happened for a reason. There was something I was supposed to learn, to explore within myself. The timing of it all and the way it all went down were not that of miracles and the unexplainable. I believe they were just part of the path I was on.

I didn't know at the time that those events were leading me here, to this moment, rolling Dad's suitcase into the Park MGM lobby, thinking of the fragility of this trip, how it could go any which way between Dad and me. If you're one of those people, like myself, who believes there are no such things as accidents, then you can see that every event in life is interconnected and has a bit of a butterfly effect to it. I stop to think about that as I listen to Dad rave about the opening monologue of conservative pundit Michael Savage on the radio during his drive to Vegas. Somehow, someway, an event like failing Finance in college and all the past arguments I had with him from the time I was a teenager to now has led to a moment like this, watching the elevator increase in floor numbers, him talking with his hands about the economy and the state of the military. I ended up here with him. I guess that is a miracle in its own right.

=====

We head to the sportsbook to place our bets for college football. When Dad bets on football, he doesn't research or look at anything. He doesn't listen to sports podcasts or radio analysts giving their insights into the matchups. He barely watches the pundits on ESPN College Gameday provide their analyses on the spread, and he doesn't use a phone app to read any articles. Nothing. He grabs a betting sheet and a pen from the betting counter and spends no more than twenty-five minutes circling the teams he likes. He then looks over his sheet using his pen to double-check his choices and with a slight nod in agreement of what he has landed on, he heads to the betting counter with a stack of twenties in his hands.

I've watched him use this process since he brought me to Vegas for the first time—around the age of ten. I would have to stand far off, on the main carpet, since I was underage, and he would go bet on football games, telling me to wait right outside the sportsbook so he could see me.

Dad's process for betting games is quite fascinating, and I admire his loyalty to it. He's a man of routine, a creature of habit. "If it ain't broke, don't fix it" is a favorite quote of his. Dad and I have been betting on football for as long as I can remember. He taught me how to read point spreads, what to look for in an offense and defense, and the impact the weather has on the points total for the game.

He leaves the betting window, his tickets in hand. I ask him what games he landed on and if he is going to bet anymore today.

"Nope, I got who I wanted. Now, let's enjoy the rest of the day."

Dad wins twelve out of the thirteen football games he bet on. Twelve out of thirteen! How in the world did he do that? To win more than you lose, even by the slightest margin is considered a good day, especially in Vegas where the city is designed for you to lose everything you own. Dad lost one game the entire day, and man, does he parade his butt off when we get back to the room! He struts around, his chest puffed out a bit. He jokingly declares he is a betting genius, that he has outsmarted the books.

Despite his incredible night, Dad brings himself back to earth, claiming that Vegas is the great equalizer to a man's ego.

"It'll humble you real fast," he says.

He sits on the bed and takes his shoes off and readies to pour himself a cup of wine, still laughing in disbelief that he lost only one football game. And I am pretty proud of my performance, hitting seven out of twelve games for wins. Not too shabby leaving Vegas with more money in my pocket than when I arrived.

Dad flips the channel to the second half of the prime-time evening Pac-12 football game. He stays silent, sipping his wine, his left sock showing the beginnings of a hole over his ankle bone. I watch him at ease, his eyes drifting narrower with the slow-paced offense on television.

"Dad, can I ask you something?"

"Yes, son."

"How the hell did you do it?"

"Do what?"

"Twelve out of thirteen games? That's unheard of."

He starts laughing in disbelief. "Well, ya know, God felt like I deserved a little today."

"Seriously, Dad," I replied. "How did you do it?"

Dad's a history buff. Always has been. His bookshelf contains Churchill, World War II, and conservative authors retelling the patterns of America's past as demonization of its future. Rarely does he read anything outside of those topics. He's meticulous in his reading. He never went digital. The feeling of paper and the binding of a book in the palms of his hands is something he enjoys.

When he would sit in the sauna at the gym, he would bring a book with him, hunched over, consuming each line. It is a daily practice for him. Some days, it is ten pages; others, he reads for hours. And whatever he reads, he shares it immediately with whoever is in close proximity. At times, he'll send me a picture of a passage from the Daily Bread, adding a caption to it. I see the similarities between us with our reading habits. We both enjoy the feel of books, the weight of them in our hands. And we both love to share what we just read with whoever is around us.

Dad adjusts himself into a more upright position on the bed, his eyes fixated on the current play before turning his vision toward me.

"It's easy to bet games when you've watched the same team for the last twenty years, running the same offense, having the same demeanor they've always had. Culture is built from the get-go. The moment a school is established, they already have taken on a personality."

He mentions the old-school nature of Stanford and Wisconsin, two of his favorite teams. He describes how the schools have histories of breeding offensive lineman the size of SUVs with the footwork of professional ballet dancers. Dancing bears is what the scouts in the NFL call those guys. He talks about Penn State, how they are always able to have a linebacker or two who could run through a brick wall and have hands that could catch anything thrown their way. He goes into the rivalries, a key component in his methodology of betting.

"You have to remember the way teams play each other," he says. "College football is all emotion. It's all passion. That all dies out when guys get to the pros. They're making big money now. Sure, they get more amped up closer to the playoffs, but college is all about the students, the school. You're playing for something much bigger than you. You're playing for tradition, for legacy."

"So you just remember teams that don't like each other and how they play against one another, and that's your strategy?" I ask him.

"Pretty much. Sometimes you win; sometimes you lose. Every once in a while, you get a day like this where you leave Vegas with a little cash in your pocket."

He sips his wine then places it on the nightstand between our beds as the game winds down. I start to undress, rummaging through my suitcase for a pair of basketball shorts.

"Hey, Dad, did you happen to see where my blue shorts went?"

He doesn't respond to me as I move my hand through the bottom of my luggage. I turn around to see his eyes are closed, his legs crossed, his hands clasped on top of his stomach, and I hear a slight snore echoing through his nose. I smile.

"Night, Dad. See you in the morning."

———

Vegas on Sunday morning is quite reminiscent of what it was before the COVID pandemic—small groups of people, from a night out, booze still in their systems, swaying back and forth as they enter the Starbucks in the Cosmopolitan Hotel. There are men with their dress shirts untucked, women with their heels in hand, walking barefoot on the Vegas pavement, passing a group of motivators dressed in their running clothes, getting their daily cardio.

Dad and I laugh at the scenery before us as we drive through the Strip on our way to Sebring. It hits me in the first five minutes of this ride that I feel stuck with him, trapped within the confines of the Mercedes van, alone with a man who I have not forgiven. A feeling of regret swells up inside of me, similar to the feelings I had when I stood feet away from the famed yellow footprints of Marine Corps Bootcamp and minutes before I had to plant my two feet on top of a set. Before those events, I had told my friends how stoked I was to go, to fight in a war for my country. I bragged to my mom that I would be fine and promised I wouldn't die with words that held no guarantee. I remember telling Dad how I believed that Bootcamp was going to show everyone what I'm made of. He said he had no doubt I would quickly learn what I was capable of. He told me not to quit, to give myself a chance to make something of myself. That was the one and only time he had offered me advice that really resonated with me. It stuck with me all through those thirteen weeks of blood, sweat, and tears. It was something I thought about while sitting on top of a gun turret, driving through Iraq during my tours of duty. But it was also something I forgot when I came home and discovered I am still mad at him.

While we laugh at the drunks and hard-chargers running the infamous boulevard of broken dreams, I think of those words he said to me. I think of how this car ride with him will show me if anything between us will ever be different or if it will be the same run-of-the-mill, shallow relationship it has always been.

Whatever the feeling, the regret and anxiety of driving east to Arizona are weighing on me. I feel the urge to look up a flight that'll take me back to Denver as we pass McCarran International Airport. I stuff my face full of M&Ms with the hope the blend of chocolate and peanut butter will bring me some peace and tranquility. But then I remember what Dad told me before I left for Bootcamp.

"Don't quit, son. Show them what you're made of."

And that's when I realize that Dad has known me my entire life. He has known me from the moment I came into this world. He has seen me grow from a young boy into a teenager and then into a man. He has watched me fail. He's seen me succeed. He has seen my heart get broken. He has seen the pieces of it get put back together.

But I have not known Dad for his entire life. I have only known him as a father, and my viewpoint of him has only been how he performs as one. I don't know what he was like before I was born. I don't know what he went through as a young man fresh out of college. I don't know what kept him up at night. I have no idea what was emotionally stirring inside of him when he left my mom and had to start over as a single man with two kids and only part-time custody. I have no clue what he was thinking when he started his businesses. There is so much I did not know of him. Maybe that's why we used to fight. Maybe that's why I have built up this resentment toward him. We have thousands of miles to go, and the voice I heard when he first called me to go on this trip comes again.

"Michael, ask your dad about his life."

I sat with the voice again, just like I did on that call. I inhale a couple of deep breaths, pursing the air out through my mouth, and then I swallow my fear, the fear that tells me we're only a handful of miles into this trip and it's as good as it's going to get between us. I put aside the agony of my youth, the days and years of not speaking to him, and I ask, "Dad, what were you like before I was born?"

WHEN ALL YOUR FRIENDS ARE GONE

There is a ray of sunshine bouncing off the copper-toned scenery of New Mexico, creating a subtle light that reflects onto the road. It wakes me up a little bit. When I asked Dad about his life, it was a loaded question. The man has lived and been through more than I can comprehend. He's loved and lost multiple times. He's won and lost at business. He's lost God, and he's found him again. I was expecting Dad to tell me something funny. Guy humor if you will. Instead, he drops a bomb on me.

"Bill from church passed away the other day." Dad takes the palm of his right hand off the steering wheel and wipes it on his pants. He says this with a somberness and surrealness that he understands he's in the back nine of his life.

"No kidding, from what?"

"Cancer. He had it for a long time."

He stares off into the distance toward a gas station with a couple of cars and an old wooden sign reading Petrol. The rubber hitting the road between us creates a white noise effect. I want to pry further, curious to hear Dad's thoughts on mortality as he's living out his golden years. There is also a part of me that wants to pass over the subject entirely. To speak about death with him seems inappropriate. He's alive and well. He takes no meds, no prescriptions anyway, and has no cane or walker. He's in better shape than some thirty-year-olds I know. He would give most middle-aged men a run for their money when it comes to overall health. He's spry, still full of energy. For how long he will continue like this, I do not know. He does not know either.

"Bill was a good man," I told him.

"Bill was a hell of a guy. All those guys from St. Paul's. You remember them, right?"

When I was a kid, Dad would take my brother and me to this church in Healdsburg named St. Paul's. A small, quaint white-painted church that stood prominently in the middle of downtown. The outside of the church was desperately in need of a paint job, the crucifix at the top had some rust that you could see if you looked directly up at it from the entrance. Dad called St. Paul's "a place with character."

The inside of the church was magnificent. It was covered from floor to ceiling in dark stained wood. The pews were immaculately engraved with *fleurs-de-lis* on the side of the armrests. The tabernacle had a gold crucifix with stones embedded in it, and the altar—made out of white marble—had been perfectly measured and cut equally on each side. The priest, Father Marvin, was the heartbeat of the Sunday services. He sang his heart out with every homily; he preached with humility. When I would raise my hand in church to ask questions about Jesus in the middle of his sermon, Dad would give me a "what do you think you are doing" look while Father Marvin called upon me to go ahead and ask my question. He always answered them.

Whenever we walked into St. Paul's, Dad was greeted by his dear friends: Max, Bill, and Floyd. The four of them together posed as the Christian version of the infamous Rat Pack. They all wore suits in the same color scale, head to toe, pressed and clean. They would greet each other with hugs and firm handshakes. They discussed politics, news, and the memories of their youth as young college students. The handful of times I saw Dad filled with utter joy were when we were around these guys on Sunday mornings. Bill generally stood in the middle of the four men. He was even-keeled, never raising his voice in joy nor in anger. He had a pencil mustache lined up to the edges of his mouth with military precision. His hair was always parted on the right side, gelled to keep stray hairs from standing straight up. Whenever I saw Bill, he would shake Dad's hand first, then immediately grab mine. He always shook it with firmness and spoke to me as though I was a colleague of his, a rarity that adults do with young children.

As we make our way into West Texas, Dad starts talking about all the times he and Bill shared at the men's retreats hosted by their church. He shares the conversations that took place, the exchanging of ideas on how to walk biblically. He dives into aspects of their bond over Christ and conversations about their path toward God. He then grows quiet and somber when he seems to realize again that Bill is no longer here.

Minutes have gone by. We now stare at the mid-afternoon sun through the windshield.

"I'm sorry to hear about Bill, Dad. I liked him."

"Me too, son," he replies.

"What about Floyd, is he still around?"

"Oh, yeah. Floyd is on those emails I send you with the political satire jokes. You get those right?"

From time to time, Dad forwards me a thread with Floyd's email on it. Most times, I ignore them completely, in large part because they are politically charged. I'm just not into that kind of stuff. Sometimes, I read them, and I find myself reading them more frequently as I grow older in an attempt to understand Dad. What stands out to me about Floyd is his consistency. Floyd loves navy suits and his shirts were always pressed neatly every time I saw him. His hands are strong, a gold ring prominently displayed as a married man. His mustache rivals Tom Selleck's and makes it easy to pick him out of a crowd. These days, Floyd and Dad talk when time permits. Dad mentions Floyd is alive and well, and I'm glad to hear he still has a deep friendship into his old age that stems from his days at St. Paul.

"Max passed away some time ago, right?" I ask.

Dad adjusts his sunglasses. Max is somewhat of a sensitive spot for my dad. Max was at the top of his list when it came to role models, men of prominence and stature.

Dad speaks of Max in the same breath he speaks of General Patton and John Wayne.

"Oh, yeah. Max has been gone for some time. He was an outstanding man. I mean, they don't make them like they used to when it came to Max."

I gravitated toward Max the most of Dad's friends when I was a kid on Sunday mornings. Nothing was ever out of place with Max. His suit and pants were pressed, not a wrinkle on them. He wore just enough gold on his hands and fingers to show you he was a man of notoriety but also of humility and family. His hair was neat and all in alignment, the same silver and white color of Gandalf The Great from *Lord of the Rings*. And he was like this every single time I saw him. His energy and presence were something else. He shook your hand with grace and softness, his eyes connecting to yours as though you were the only thing that mattered at the moment. Max's smile was so big and wide, you could see the silver fillings in the back of his teeth. He strolled through the church making his rounds with everyone with his wife beside him like he was a mayoral candidate. He always gave back to his community; he stayed married to the same woman until his death. He was a man that Dad, in his old age, continues to aspire to be.

Dad speaks of Max as a man that truly knew what it meant to leave his mark on the world. Dad's relationship with him was special. When Max started to decline with age, Dad went to see him a lot. Max would be wrapped in a blanket, sitting by a warm fire, on his last winter nights, staring into the dancing brightness of the flames. They would talk for hours, God and Jesus at the forefront of their conversations, followed by the trivialness of day-to-day life. Dad would go to Max for counsel, to help heal the brokenness of his past.

I watch now as Dad's shirt starts to become wet from his tears. He begins to speak of his self-proclaimed broken nature. He speaks of the years he spent wandering, making choices that always led him to a dead-end or the middle of nowhere. These were the periods in his life where he searched high and low for answers. He mentions that men are often the ones who wander—and wander alone—in the pursuit of their purpose. It is mandatory and a rite of passage, he says, for a man to be lost in order to be found.

Dad's pursuit of purpose started with the ups and downs of his twenties as he navigated the streets of San

Francisco during the "free love" era. He frequented the Fillmore for the live music, smoked doobies with his buddies, and lived with a wild and free heart. It was in San Francisco where he experienced true freedom, a man carving a path out for himself as a young entrepreneur.

He looks out through the driver-side window, scanning the scenery, and pauses for two breaths before continuing on. His monologue transitions into his thirties, the decade where his marriages and the wishing he knew better of what it took to be a husband took place. He says he poured himself into his work, creating the beginning of a long, successful career. At thirty-seven, he became a dad when I came into the world. I stop him in his storytelling tracks when he mentions this.

"What was it like for you when I was born?"

He collects himself, shifting his hands on the steering wheel. He purses his lips together in thought, a signature move of his for as long as I have known him, indicating he is processing what to say or attempting to troubleshoot a challenge—like the ones he ran into with his 1976 BMW 2002.

"You know, it was just me and your mom, and that was all I was worried about. It had always been just the two of us. And when your mom was pregnant with you,

I was looking forward to becoming a dad. But it didn't hit me until you were born that it was no longer just me and your mom. There were now three of us. I had a son. And that hit me hard. You were born into the world and couldn't fend for yourself. I had to provide for you and your mother now, not just for me."

For a few seconds, Dad stares at me. It is a look of a father recognizing again that he has a son. I imagine this is how he looked at me when I was born, holding me in his arms, realizing I am half of who he is. I wish to tell him that I see him clearly now, but I refrain. I quickly pivot back to his story about Max.

"Dad, finish what you were telling me about Max."

"Before I go on about Max, do you remember Russell?" he asks.

"The landlord?"

"Yeah, the guy that owned The Eagle's Nest."

Russell was my dad's landlord of The Eagle's Nest after my parents divorced. Dad claimed Russell was always hitting him up for something on his rent—a tax here, another fee there. Dad, being the numbers and money wizard he is, always made a fuss when Russell would charge him for something. And as much as Dad claimed Russell was just trying to bleed him dry, Russell was the one who brought my Dad to Bible study one evening, a night that would change his life forever.

"If it wasn't for Russell, I have no idea where I would be. I was lost, man. And Max, well, Max brought me to Jesus, and I got saved."

There are two tears that start to form in the corners of my eyes. I feel them coming on, and I try so hard to hold them back. One of them falls down the side of my face, and I quickly wipe it. Dad had lost his guiding light, his beacon, the man who found him when he needed to be found. He had lost a true friend. I start to think of the friends I have lost to suicide, drugs, and alcohol. I have lost colleagues in motorcycle accidents days after I spoke with them on the phone. Death is hard to grapple with, whether it is our own mortality that is drawing near or someone we love who disappears from the world in a snap of our fingers. I spent many nights and days wondering why my friends left far too soon. In some ways, it has been easier to accept the brevity of life. While I miss them, I know they are in a better place, no longer burdened with pain or suffering. They are at peace. Hard to come to terms with, but I try to accept it. In some ways, it is easier to deal with them being gone far too soon than what I imagine it'd feel like to lose someone after they've shared the majority of your life with you.

I have never lost a friend to old age. I have not grown old enough to have a friendship span a significant portion of my life, only to witness them erode in their final days. I have not had a friend I've known forever sit by a fire, mustering every ounce of energy to talk with me on his way to the afterlife. My dad is experiencing that in his life. His friends of many years are developing health problems, and they're all slowly making their way to eternal rest.

What helps Dad speak of his friends passing over the years with such conviction and acceptance is that he believes he will see them again in Heaven. His faith and love will be the golden tickets to the big party in the sky, a time to be with his friends again. It is a true blessing in life to listen to him talk about mortality, his mortality, and the celebration that awaits him in Heaven. Little do we ever get a glimpse of our parents in this vulnerable state during the back nine of their lives. I hear him speak of peace and calm for when it's his time to go. He envisions himself surrounded by loved ones—myself and my brothers, his wife, his grandchildren—on his way to eternal rest.

I believe this is secretly how we all wish to have our lives end. In old age, surrounded by love and joy, knowing we did everything we could to make the best use of ourselves and our time on this earth. I know it's where I wish to be. A long healthy life to reflect on and memories to serve me in the days I have left.

Dad is quiet in thought after talking about Max, about the end, about how all of his friends are gone. He directs his attention to the gray clouds in the distance, the setting sun peeking now through.

"Dad, you okay?" I ask him.

"Yeah, it's just that . . . you know . . . you miss your friends. I miss those guys. Bill and Max. I grew up with them in church. Those guys helped bring me to Christ. And, you know, they're not here anymore. It's just, um . . ."

His lip starts to quiver a bit. He adjusts his hands on the wheel yet again. He knows that time is more precious now. The days are much more valuable than they were before. His quiver turns into a smirk of gratitude. What a joy it must have been for him to spend his years running the race of life with his friends. We should all be so lucky to have a Bill and a Max in our lives, running alongside us, picking us up when we fall, pushing us when we start to tire. He wishes that he could finish what he started with them. It is now only him running.

"Son, you have your whole life ahead of you," he blurts out. "Don't waste it. Don't let it pass you by. Don't miss out on being with your friends. When I found Jesus, Bill and Max hugged me and told me how proud they were of me. We had a good ride together. Someday, I'll see them again. I know I will. And we'll all be together."

He cries as he says this, but they are tears of joy. Tears made of the memories of his friends who he keeps alive as he carries on to the end of the race. There is the sound of the wind whipping over the hood of our van, the faint organ notes of the Doors' "Riders on the Storm," playing in the background. That song is my dad's favorite song. We both stare into the golden rays shining off a road sign on the interstate.

There is a serenity that overcomes me, the conversation of life and death and brotherhood taking us through an emotional, thought-provoking rollercoaster. I feel a sense of connection, one I have not ever had with Dad before. It is one that wishes to embrace him with love and forgiveness for all the years I ignored him, hated him, and emotionally disowned him.

As we get older, the days become more precious. Moments and time fly by. We cannot be here forever; the good times come and go. Friends that brought you to your faith, the love of your life, even your career and other relationships—they will all eventually be gone. You will not be here anymore. Time catches up with all of us.

The two of us on the road together, sitting in the sunset of a badly paved interstate, driving east, the depth of what was shared filling the cabin . . . this is a moment I will never forget.

GET ON THE BUS

There is an endless stretch of highway that makes me go deep into the rabbit hole of self-examination. I think about what would happen if the proverbial rug was pulled out from underneath me and having to start over in life. I think about the end of my days, wondering whether I will have done enough to warrant a life well-lived. Questions pop up. Did I love and learn what I could? Did I help people? Did I live without regrets?

I cannot help but lose myself at times in thinking about these things, especially in the conditions of a pandemic world. We are inundated with news from every channel on TV, updating us in real-time with the case total. Morning radio talk show hosts continue to talk about COVID for as long as possible. It is hard not to think about death when it's all everyone is talking about. My body takes on the tingling sensation of fear, uncertainty, and doubt, and I look over at Dad to take my eyes off the boring stretch of land surrounding Interstate 40.

His hands are lightly caressing the steering wheel, and the brim of his ball cap sits an inch above his prescription sunglasses. He is staring out of the windshield, his eyes piercing the dirt, bugs, and dried raindrops. There are clouds in the distance, a storm approaching. Dad admires nature. He is also fearful of it. Whenever he sees something of beauty that nature provides, there is a certain look he gets. It is one of curiosity. Now, his eyes widen as he takes in the depth of the dark clouds. There are hints of gray, subtle accents that make him say, "That looks like it is going to be a big storm." Storms are his favorite parts of nature.

When I was a kid, my dad would peer out the back window at our house in Sonoma County and place his fingers on the glass, staring upward at the sky from underneath the edge of the roof. The rain would start to pour; shots of lightning bolts would touch down in the distance. Like clockwork, he would mutter, "Holy hell, it is coming down."

Thunder and lightning used to scare the crap out of me as a kid. Any time a storm would start, I'd run into my room and hide beneath the covers of my bed. Minutes later, Dad would knock on the door and tell me to come to look at the storm with him. I'd say no when he asked the first time. But he would ask me again, and reluctantly, I'd move out from underneath the covers, halfway committing to watching the storm with him but very much afraid too. He would ask me again, this time opening the door, waving his hands at me. I'd shift my feet to the ground and walk to the back of the house near the back-door's glass pane, the only thing separating Dad and me from the ferocity of the thunderstorm.

"Man, how powerful this thing is!" he'd say. "You see the rain coming down?"

I'd nod slowly and reply "yes," my hands pressing against the glass. We'd sit in the special silence of the pounding rain and rumbling thunder. As much as I was still afraid, I felt a sense of comfort too, knowing Dad was beside me.

I had forgotten those memories with him up until now, watching this storm approaching us, the wipers slapping back and forth, brushing the drops of water off the windshield. The clouds above remind me of all the storms that came and went—not just at our house but in my life. I tell him—as the storm ahead rages on—that my life thus far has been a series of winding turns and roads, less conventional than I'd imagined, and it's made me feel that I am behind the eight ball in many ways. I tell him that the season of life I'm in makes me feel that marriage and family are not in the cards for me. The anxiety I felt in the weeks and days before sharing with him my deepest troubles bubble within me, and a huge pause creates a gap in communication.

Then, I share that I am afraid I am not cut out for entrepreneurship, that I am more of a failure than a success. I continue to ramble on about my perceptions and worries, losing myself in thinking about all the things I wish I could do over again: college, relationships, career choices. I have a habit of losing myself in thinking about these things. At times, this habit further complicates being in the present as I often think about the future and the uncertainties that lie within it. Here I sit, worried about my future, and Dad is as cool as the other side of a pillow. I wonder if he's listening to me at all as I air my grievances. He is focusing on the road and staring at the rain clouds up above through the windshield. He mutters to himself, and I hear enough to make out his admiration for the eye of the storm.

"You know, Michael, I went through the same stuff you did." He breaks the momentary silence with the unwrapping of a pack of Ricola cough drops as he says this. He offers me one, and I take it.

"You did?" I ask.

"Oh, yeah, I did. Man, when I was your age, I had no effin' clue what the hell I was doing. I still don't!"

He laughs, the rattling of a hard cough drop brushing up against his molars.

"I'm going to tell you something. Ever since you were a kid, I've always told you that you would be a great entrepreneur. And you have already learned the most valuable lesson of entrepreneurship, which is that you will get knocked off your feet. You will feel like you failed every single day. And you will get up. You will clean yourself off. And you'll get back at it."

The cough drop in my own mouth has a weird taste to it, a mix of echinacea and mint honey. I can't figure out if I like it or hate it. Yet, I start to feel a sense of calm from sucking on it, a relief mixed with caution as I heed Dad's prophetic words.

"Listen, as for the family, marriage thing. Your father is not one to call himself an expert, but I'll tell you that it will all fall in place when you meet the right woman. And you'll know. And you don't want to rush it. Trust me. When it does happen for you, being a dad is one of the best things I have ever done."

I almost choke on my cough drop. *What did he just say?* Being a dad is one of the best things he's ever done?

"You alright?" he asks me, a concerned look on his face.

"Yeah, I'm straight." I collect myself, pulling out the wrinkles on my shirt as though it hadn't seen an iron in years.

"And the business part of your life and what you're doing. Everyone that runs their own business goes through failure. That's part of the game, especially in the agency business. The setbacks, the clients being on you 24/7. I used to have days in the ad agency where I hoped we could make payroll. I had nights where I was up worrying about where the next paycheck would come from. I worried about how we were going to get out of debt, make more money. Recessions. Presidents. You name it. I have seen it all."

The rain hits harder. Small waves of water stream behind the cars in front of us on the freeway. The thunder strengthens, and when combined with the noise of the rain, it's almost ironic for this conversation.

"Dad, I feel like I'm grasping at straws. I worry so much about—"

"You got to stop worrying," he interrupts me. "That's the problem. You're thinking too much about what has happened and what may happen. You're not thinking about *now*. Now is the time for you to do something. You got to get on the bus, Michael. Just do it. Don't overthink it. You'll adjust to whatever happens. The worst thing you can do is sit still worrying. You got to trust that God is going to take care of you. The pieces will come together and everything will work out when you just do it. If you want to be successful and that is what you want—to have money, freedom, all of it—then get on the bus. If it's working, you'll adjust. If it's not working, you'll adjust. You're a smart kid, Michael. You always have been. You just gotta do it. Be like Nike. 'Just do it.'"

It was as though I had just been given a sermon, and it rocks me to my core, a personalized TED talk for an audience of one that changes everything. It was as if the words on the page of a good book hit me upside the head. Like most of us, I have been searching for answers. Something that would put my mind at ease. And here it was.

The clouds pale into a light gray. The rain softens into a mist. The traffic starts to clear.

"Thanks, Dad. I needed to hear that."

"Don't mention it. Just do it, son. I know you can."

There is a silence between us as I digest his mantra of getting on the bus. Our exit is twenty miles ahead.

THE ETERNAL PARTY

My dad loves singing in church. He can't sing to save his life, but man, you can never fault him for a lack of effort. When he took me to church as a kid, he would gently hit my shoulder with the back of his hand if I wasn't singing as loud as he was. I'd look up, and he'd give me a flash of a smile and wait for me to join in, harmonizing with him. My stepmother would sometimes look at us as jokers, two guys making a good time out of a Psalm. Dad would laugh a little, look down at me, and give a nod.

Make no mistake, Dad reveres church as his personal sanctuary. Throughout his life, it is where he found healing when he was broken. It is where he found a community of men and prayer. The joys of faith, and the conviction that we all must believe in something bigger than ourselves. Singing in church is Dad's way of reaffirming his faith.

I never understood church as a kid: the singing, the praying, the praise to something I couldn't see. I considered my time at church on Sundays to be a form of torture as a young Mike Liguori, a boy who had the attention span of a moth and dreamed of playing in the NBA. I was more focused on counting the minutes until I could go back home and watch TV or play basketball in the backyard and work on my three-point shot. But when Dad would brush up against my shoulder in church, encouraging me to sing my butt off with him . . . those are the moments I remember, the ones that make me realize how special this trip is.

The two of us make it to Sebring, Florida, having experienced conversations about life that now, I wish we would have had sooner. The moments singing with him in church flash across my eyes as we sit together eating a medley of cooked broccoli, salmon, and rice over a Coleman grill Dad has had with him longer than I have been on the earth. The night air is starting to fill with smoke from neighboring barbeques and tunes by the Marshall Tucker Band. Dad has always been perfectly happy sitting in silence when eating and camping. He never was one to encourage playing music while we ate outside. When my brother and I would throw something on our Sony CD players as kids, Dad would tell us to turn that stuff off and utter his most famous line:

"Make pretend you're camping."

Make pretend you're camping is Dad's way of saying "suck it up buttercup." I don't know where he came up with it, but any time my brother and I started complaining about our tents being wet or sitting in the ambiance of the Sierra Nevada forest for far too long—longer than two young boys could tolerate—Dad would turn around and remind us to pretend we're camping.

Dad's got a special bond with the outdoors. In his younger years, he spent a lot of time camping, hanging with his husky named Peaches. They went all over the place, the two of them in Dad's Ford Bronco that he had up until a couple of years ago. He clocked around half a million miles in that thing, and when he finally decided it was time to stop driving it, I watched a piece of him die with its retirement.

I ask him as we eat dinner about his time camping with Peaches.

"Peaches was the best dog," he says. "We went everywhere together. I had her since she was a puppy. You remember her?"

"Of course, I do. She was great. I remember I would try to ride her as a kid."

"Oh, yeah . . . you used to get on her back, and she would let you ride for a little bit until she was over it."

He laughs a bit, gathering together a small forkful of salmon and broccoli.

"Can I ask you something, Dad?"

"Sure, what is it?"

"When you were talking about Max, you said something about a man looking for his purpose, having to be lost before he could be found. You never told me what you were looking for."

"What was I looking for? Jeez, I don't know. I don't even remember—it was so long ago."

"Was it God, Heaven, life? What was it?"

Dad has a mouthful of food, chuckling a bit as he chomps away. "You gotta ask me this right now, as I'm eating?"

"I was just curious, that's all."

He continues to chew his food—broccoli half-chewed, a piece of rice is caught on his chin and he doesn't know it's there. I motion to him where it is. He swipes at it, and it falls to the ground.

"I don't know what I was looking for, to be honest. But I didn't know I was looking for anything until I found it."

"Well, what about God and Heaven? You were looking for that, right?"

"Looking for God and Heaven just happens to be a part of it. Now that I think of it, I was actually looking for my invite to the eternal party—as we all are according to Father Marvin."

"Do you think people are just partying up in Heaven . . . like, the whole time?" I ask, eyebrows raised.

"I mean, yeah. What else do you think is happening up there? They ain't working at a desk, I'll tell you that much."

He laughs to himself, taking another bite. He used to feel uncomfortable talking about the party in the sky— the slight uneasiness of talking about *the end*. As I have watched Dad grow older, I've noticed he's begun to speak of Heaven as a means of surrendering, letting go of the ultimate control . . . that our time is decided by something much bigger than our existence.

"You know, I think of Heaven as a huge resort. St. Peter waiting at the gates for you like a concierge at a five-star hotel. Nice white robes and a huge book with everyone's name on it. And when it's your turn to meet Him, he takes his pen and looks for you in the ledger."

"What do you think he'll do when you go up there, Dad?" I asked him.

"Well, I just think he'll look at me and go, 'Mr. Liguori, we've been expecting you. We have your room ready and prepared in the Ivory Tower on the twenty-fifth floor—with a view.'"

I laugh at his description of a heavenly penthouse with his name on the door, a pure gold placard engraved with *James Liguori*, the idea of an ivory tower at the country club of Heaven. Yet, it is also devastating to hear this, the sheer thought that someday, he will not be here with me. It is surreal to be here with him now, talking about the afterlife, the part after the end. I understand this is a moment with him I'll never have again. The two of us sitting underneath the moonlight of a humid Florida night, the collision of country music on one side of the infield and 80s hair metal on the other, meeting in the middle of our campground.

Dad is content where he is right now. He looks up at the stars, raising his eyebrows, and squinting in an effort to see the heavens better.

"What do you think God is, Dad?" I ask him. My hands are covered in sweat and oil from the cooked salmon that fell onto my pants that I retrieved a moment ago. I wipe them on the tablecloth.

"I can't explain God to you. I don't even understand God. It's unexplainable what He is, what He's created. The universe. Nature. Humans. It's so complicated . . . how could you possibly fathom to know how and why it exists?"

"I agree with you. I can't either. But you don't think he's an old man, sitting in a chair with white robes?"

He laughs and pauses to wipe his mouth.

"No, of course not. You know, Einstein said the more he tried to understand the universe, the more he realized he couldn't."

"Did Einstein believe in God?"

He sits then adjusts himself in his seat, moving his butt from one spot on the bench to six inches over.

"I would imagine so. You can't go that deep into the universe without stumbling upon the existence of God," he said.

I stop to think for a moment. It is in our noble curiosity that we find something bigger in the midst of trying to understand something much larger than ourselves. The inner workings of gravity, the way mountains formed and stood miles above sea level, my dad mentioning during the eighties and his ad agency days, that there were days where money just came right into the company accounts when they exactly needed it to get through the month. He continues his commentary and I watch him revel in finding common ground with arguably one of the most recognizable scientists in human history. He smiles in satisfaction that he and Einstein recognize God in the unexplainable.

I ask him what he regrets in his life, a quick pivot away from the metaphysical.

"Michael, I have many regrets. I have many things I wish I did differently. But life goes on. You make mistakes. You live with them. You can only go forward, not backward. It does you no good holding onto them. One regret I do have is that I wish I wouldn't have gotten married so many times. Would have saved me a lot of money and heartache."

He chuckles then downs a sip of wine and takes a bite of his food, with a look of slight contemplation and satisfaction, knowing that he has a suite up in Heaven with his name on the door.

"Well, considering the number of times you have gone to church and prayed, I'm sure St. Peter and God won't hold your marriages against you," I joke.

"I sure hope not," he says. "Otherwise, there goes my penthouse suite."

12 HOURS OF SEBRING

Sebring has a calm-before-the-storm feel to it. I peer through the back of the van—where I slept last night—watching Dad breathe in the silence of the morning, a cup of coffee in one hand as he stares at the ground. His right hand graces his hip. I've always wondered what he thinks about when he takes his signature stance in the early hours of the morning. That stance of his has been a mainstay in all the years I have known him. On every trip he's taken me on, almost every morning, he stands off in a semi-wide open space and in silence. Doesn't say a word, always looking out into the scenery or focusing on the ground in front of him. The man has been through a lot and experienced more in his lifetime than I realized prior to this trip. He's shared with me moments of pain, joy, and other realities he has lived through. I assume that the moments he shared with me on our trip to Sebring are the things he's thinking about this morning. Perhaps he's reflecting on his past, maybe (or not) wishing he could do it all over again. His face is calm, his lips pursed in the mugginess of a Florida morning. I treasure this moment of watching him. He looks content. He looks like he's at peace.

After a while, I open the van door, and he turns his head, flashing me a smile the moment he sees my face.

"Good morning, son."

"Hey, Dad."

"Today is race day. You're going to love it."

"Yeah, I am curious to see what it's about. Looking forward to it."

For as long as I have known him, Dad has been fascinated by modern machinery. Speed to him is another form of imagination coming to life. We are always going faster than we were before. He loves knowing that every year, humans find a way to go faster . . . and then faster still. Auto racing quenches his thirst. He could watch racing all day. The people, the time, the speed, the drive of competition. A novice admirer of auto racing has trouble understanding how it all works in unison. He doesn't, though. He sees every part as a contribution to breaking barriers. It is the ultimate test of human reflex and coordination. It is mysticism and unexplainable, and I have a hard time wrapping my head around what racing means to him. But I don't have to understand. According to him, the most beautiful things are unexplainable. They possess a spiritual nature, a soul or spirit that makes the inanimate animate. It makes the living feel more vibrant, connected. And we're not supposed to get how and why it works that way. We're just supposed to acknowledge its existence.

Thirty-plus cars zig and zag on the beaten pavement, heat emanating from the engine compartments. Fans sit and stand sporadically throughout. Some have masks on; some are dangling, and some are placed over chins. Every one of the fans in attendance is excited that a difficult year could not deter a great race from happening. The capacity at Sebring is not as full as it used to be in years past, but it is enough to give you an idea of how rocking this place would be at its max. Dad tells me that before the pandemic, this place could hold 250,000 screaming race fans, trailers, and RVs to the brim with people. There is nonstop partying in turns #3 and #13. There are people of all ages, all walks of life, sitting on lawn chairs or standing and holding their intricate cameras, snapping pictures of cars banking turns at speeds in the triple digits.

I am quite amazed at the first couple of laps in the race. The roar of the exhaust and motors rivaling those of commercial jetliners. There are early battles for the top three positions. Dad is locked in on the BMW race team—a team he's been cheering for longer than I have been alive. I ask him why he loves BMW so much.

"Engineering is at its finest with BMW. I kind of fell in love with them when I bought the 1976 2002 in the garage. It just became something I started to give my time to. Working on it. Driving it. You remember riding in it, don't you?"

"I do. Not very clearly but enough to know you always drove it carefully and never really drove it fast," I say.

"What would I need to do that for? It's a BMW; they're meant to be enjoyed, cruised around in."

He pulls a bit on the brim of the BMW motorsport cap he wears with the pride of a rookie drafted by a professional sports team. His smile beams from ear to ear as he wears the BMW logo. I know the feeling. I was once a young Marine recruit, stepping on the yellow footprints of Marine Corps Recruit Depot San Diego. For thirteen weeks, you bury yourself in mud and sand. You go days with limited sleep. You live your life under a microscope and are trained to fight and kill. A lack of violence and aggression is not allowed. Make it to the end of training and you find yourself in formation, at attention on a parade deck in San Diego, hand out, ready to receive the legendary "Eagle, Globe, and Anchor," which few have had the privilege of wearing. That emblem in your hand becomes much more than a logo. You've *earned* it. You deserve it. You put yourself through the wringer to call yourself a Marine.

Rookies get that feeling when they're drafted. Guys like my dad get that feeling when they spend years of their life pouring into a team, following every race day. Dad mentions that the indoctrination into racing begins with the car you buy and work on. The hours turning wrenches, studying its intake system. You fix what needs to be fixed. You surf the online forums for answers to a headlight, find aftermarket parts on a German auto site to throw a little juice in the motor. Both your relationship with your car and to the community are bred, in other words, out of a labor of love. Dad has spent forty-plus years working tirelessly on his '76 BMW 2002. He's still building it today. He is not a young rookie drafted by an NFL team or a young boy stepping into manhood on the grounds of Marine Corps Recruit Depot San Diego. He is a fan—a man whose most precious commodity, that of *time*, has been given to the pursuit of auto-racing glory.

He is, in other words, part of their team. He wears the BMW logo with the pride I once had wearing the fatigues or dress uniform of a Marine. We have that in common.

———

A couple of hours into the race, Dad decides to move from the stands and drift to the BMW motorsports tent. He peers through the chain-link fence, squinting behind his glasses to analyze the screens filled with charts, bars, and real-time data trickling in from the car. It takes a team of more than twenty-five people and a couple of drivers to participate in a race of this magnitude, on a day like this. He hits me on the shoulder, pointing out a group of men looking at a screen, talking and nodding. Dad explains that a team of engineers must all be in unison, in complete sync. He gestures to one member of the team, in particular, sticking what looks like a thermometer into a set of tires that came off a car that just made a pit stop. The young man looks the most junior of the team, assigned the most tedious of tasks, while the senior members stand, watching the race from a TV.

"Is it like that everywhere?" I ask Dad.

"What do you mean?"

"The kid. I'm assuming he's the youngest, so he gets the crap jobs."

"I don't know if I would call that a crap job. We all got to pay our dues though, right? I mean you started at the bottom, too, didn't you?"

More times than you can imagine, I think.

"Yeah," I reply instead.

"Well, kid is earning his stripes. May look like a crap job to you, but to him, it's the door to his dreams. I mean, he knows he's not going to be doing that forever. He knows that. Look how much he has to pay attention to every little detail of the tire. And then he's got to go talk to the tire vendor about what he's seeing. Every little thing counts. He knows that. That's what you have to have, working in auto racing *and* in your work. Attention to detail. And you gotta love it."

A lot of us hope—and some of us expect—to shoot to the top as fast as possible. We're looking for the quickest way to become the leader. And along the way, we forget that the secret to getting to the top is paying attention to the little things . . . and that you gotta love it. Without those skills and that attitude, you'll find yourself stuck in a pattern of going through the motions, trapped in the rat race. You'll be checking all the tires and hating the fact that you're doing it.

===

Halfway through the race, we find ourselves on the other side of the track, headed back toward camp to eat. Dad is known in our family for his signature peanut butter, honey, and banana sandwiches. He's switched to almond butter in recent years, but his sandwiches are still clutch. He pulls out a couple of slices of bread, asks me if I want one. I tell him sure. I've been watching him make his famous sandwiches since I was a kid. From the many early morning treks to the ski resorts of Lake Tahoe to camping trips at Kennedy Meadows, his sandwiches were integral to any journey we took together. He finishes mine first, just like he did when I was a kid, telling me to pull up a chair and take a load off. So I do.

He makes his and sarcastically chirps, "Is it to your liking, master?"

I laugh and nod. He grabs his sandwich and has a seat next to me, untying his New Balance trail shoes and letting his feet breathe underneath blankets of white cotton. As the sun shines directly on the back of my neck and on his face, we sit in the ambient noise of racing. I have been mad at him for so long, I forgot what it was like to just be in his company in simple moments like this. As a kid, my dad and I sat among ambient noises but in the same silence, whether nature's noises were a river flowing in the background or the falling of snow onto the ground next to us—ones only we could hear.

And every once in a while, on those ski trips, we could hear the ski patrol blowing up an avalanche in the background. My father would retort, "That's a good one." I've missed these moments with him for so long. He and I sitting here, peaceful and quiet, eating our sandwiches. No longer is it him and me as father and child, sitting in the landscapes of the past. We sit now as two men getting to know each other beyond titles. It is a surreal moment, watching Dad sit the same way he always has, eating his food, staring at the ground beneath him, and pondering God knows what.

When I was younger, he'd murmur to himself about work, then seconds of silence would pass before he would utter "Ah, I see," like he had solved the mysteries of the universe rather than a problem at work. At times, he would listen intently to the radio playing in the background and when I would engage him in conversation, he would stick his hand up to quiet me as he waited to hear more of the prophetic words of Rush Limbaugh or Michael Savage.

At this moment, my dad sits the same way, only the days of Rush are no longer around. Michael Savage's radio hour has passed. He is not muttering underneath his breath while trying to sort something out. He sits in tranquil silence. I recognize now how much we are alike. I sit like he does, I mutter to myself like he once did, still trying to figure everything out in the silence of eating sandwiches.

In an endurance race, it takes a small village to keep a car in the race. Dad's favorite part has always been the amount of effort and teamwork it takes to make a car run. To achieve speeds of over 130 mph takes up to twelve people on the pit crew, another ten watching a bevy of monitors, and then another eight to ten who are spaced out between the shop and the floor. It's quite impressive. The amount of teamwork it takes to win a race, or even compete in one, is something we don't see often elsewhere. It's ironic because my dad describes himself as a lone wolf—comfortable with entertaining himself for long hours while working on his car, or as he puts it, messing around in his garage. For years, he's spoken little of team and more about individuality.

"A man is in control of his own life," he still says. "He is in control of his choices, his mission. A man is born into this world alone, and he will die alone. Along the way, he will meet people and do things with them. But at his end, he will meet his Maker alone." This is how my dad views the world.

Yet, he cheers for football teams. He watches team sports. He leads his employees at work with the same prowess Vince Lombardi had walking the sidelines for the

Green Bay Packers. He marvels as we pass the pit crews again, noticing the synchronicity and poise they possess with just a few hours left in the race. He points out to me that my brothers and I are all part of the same gene pool and blood. We might as well be in it together (*it* being life without him). I used to imagine a life without him in it. I wondered what and how I will act, a man without his father in the world for the rest of his lifetime. No more safety net, no more guidance from situations only a father knows. Sons seek wisdom from their fathers no matter how screwed up the relationship is or not. Men still want their father around for life.

Walking around the racetrack, I notice I have inherited much from him in the past days being in his presence. His love for building things, his fascination with the little things, his wonder of the cosmos, and how humanity is able to reach them. I also notice that I have inherited his curses and detriments, the hard-headedness and stubborn attitude, the notion I have all the answers simply by being in solitude and thinking, and that I do not need anyone else to figure out my problems. In essence, I inherited his "my way or the highway" mentality, his uncanny ability to grind you down into doing things how he sees fit. These are things I notice in my body, my hands gripping the chords on my backpack as he narrates the history of the track, the strategy of how the drivers are now looking for any opportunity to gain an edge over their opponents. I feel tension in my stomach, and the sweat on my hands creates a slight glaze over the plastic ends of the shoulder straps. But I am surprisingly calm. I am at peace with what I feel being around him. I am flawed in the same ways as him, but it's also binding me to him in the most spiritual of ways as the two of us wander around the racetrack as the sun sets.

We decide to move to our original location for the last thirty minutes left in The 12 Hours of Sebring. Dad is enraptured by it. I'm watching him bounce back and forth between TV screens and the finish line. He's invested—particularly in the BMW team—now more than he has been all day. One lap he awards them an *Atta boy*, the next lap he gives them a *Go faster you piece of crap*. I can't help but laugh. Watching him at seventy-four-years-old, pace back and forth—like an expecting parent in the waiting room, like a high school senior waiting to see if they landed the lead role in the fall semester play—is reinvigorating for a late-thirties guy who has been searching his whole life for something to pace about.

The Marines and a handful of tours of duty gave me adrenaline for four years and a couple after. Writing my first book and publishing it gave me a little juice also. But this is different. Dad personally knew no one on the team he is cheering for. No one. Not even the food runner. He is cheering for a car he has in his garage, a manufacturer in a country he's never been to. He was dedicated to the cause, the mission, the thrill of the final laps. After all of his years of fandom, a championship, a place on the top of the podium, is the reward. That's all he ever asked for. It's all he wants.

He continues to pace back and forth, removing his hat from his brow to wipe off the condensation of worry. I ask him what he thinks and in classic Dad fashion, he waves me off with a "shh, shh" pursuing through his mouth. He's muttering to himself at this point. At the racetrack, his behavior is acceptable and welcomed by fellow BMW and race fans alike. Outside of the confines of Sebring International Speedway, the cops and paramedics would have shown up in a split second.

It's the final laps of the race. In the middle of the last three, the black BMW—the proud stallion of the stable—spins out and winds up off the track in turn #3. I have seen my dad angry many times in my life, mostly from my behavior in grade school and high school. But disappointment is something else. I've seen him shake his head in such disbelief, bewildered, wondering what could lead to such an outcome. I have been on the receiving end of these gestures. So have my brothers. To watch his precious team lose a prestigious race such as Sebring in the final laps due to a spin-out creates a heartbreak I have never seen before though.

Fireworks start to go off in the distance, the winning team hugs and there is high-fiving all around. Through it all, my dad has a thousand-yard stare. He whispers in devastation, "How in the hell?" There is a silence and then suddenly, he snaps out of it.

"Oh, well," he says to me. "Can't win them all, right?"

My dad has said that line more times than I can count. He used to utter that line when we went to the horse track, when I was as a kid, at Bay Meadows, mostly when a longshot didn't hit like he had hoped. He said it at times when I was ten and my little league team was two innings away from winning the championship before an onslaught of runs started to pile up, and we lost badly. He even said that to me when I experienced my first heartbreak, my first girlfriend and I met during church camp at the age of fifteen. We met on a Sunday, started dating on Tuesday, and broke up that Friday night. I told my dad about it on the car ride home. My juvenile heart sat in shambles, thinking all was lost and I would never find love again. My dad knows heartbreak better than anyone.

"Oh, well," he had said. "You can't win them all, son. You'll be fine."

That car ride home was bleak. Real bleak. But he was right. I got over it. I moved on. To this day, that story of church camp is nothing more than one I share with buddies at sports bars. He knew something at the time that comes with age and experience that my teenage heart could not comprehend, nor did it want to. Life is too short and fragile to hold onto heartbreak and grudges. From life-changing victories to unexpected losses, feel the emotions in the moment. But then move on to the next one. Don't look back. Keep trucking ahead, knowing that things will be better than before. There will be another race. There will be another woman. There will be another opportunity.

I am learning an even larger lesson from my dad as we walk back to our campsite, the race results in the rearview: life is not meant to be done alone. Even my father—the self-described lone wolf who prefers to mess around in his garage than to go hit the links with some guys from his gym—knows this. It's why he's been a race fan for so long. He feels included, feels like he is part of a team. We have to have something to cheer for and something to look forward to. For my dad, BMW winning a race grants him a week of happiness. When they lose, it's a couple of minutes of sorrow and then back to the drawing board. I hadn't fully understood what his thing with racing was all about until the final laps of today's race. It's a metaphor for life. *Have something to cheer for.* Be a part of a team. Make yourself and others feel included in life. Celebrate the victories, cuss in defeat. Whatever the result, the race goes on. The season continues. On to the next track.

Life's a race anyway. Might as well run it.

ROCKET SHIP

At eight years old, I dreamed about what it would be like to see a rocket launch straight into the atmosphere, disappearing into the intersection of earth and space. I thought often about it in my front yard, mimicking the G force and propulsion of the engine. I thought about how I would be so close to the rocket, when I witnessed my first launch ever, that I would feel the vibration of the engine roaring, the rumbling of petrol burning. The flames would create a backward volcano underneath the rocket as it lifted against the laws of gravity into space. It would be one of the most impressive things I'd ever witnessed, and I thought about it all the time.

The Friday evening before the race, Dad and I were eating that campfire dinner cooked over a propane Coleman grill. He stood up in excitement, holding his phone in his left hand, using his right index finger to scan the screen. His eyes were huge as he read.

"Holy crap. You are not going to believe this!"

"What, Dad? What is it?"

"Are you ready for this? Are you ready for what I am about to read?"

Any time Dad has something exciting to read or share, he postures and poises himself to be the best hype man he can be. He did it when he announced one of my brother's birthdays was coming up. He did it when we were set to take the chair lift at Squaw Valley all the way to the top. When we played football on Saturday mornings on the beaches of Half Moon Bay, Dad would play TV commentator to set the stage for the battle that would take place and raise it just right when his foot connected with the ball for kickoff.

"I'm ready," I told him.

He paused as his index finger scrolled up on his phone, looking at me meaningfully.

"Cocoa Beach, Florida is the best place to see a rocket launch," he read. "This Saturday, SpaceX will be launching a rocket . . . Michael, I have been wanting to see a rocket launch since I was a kid."

He got quiet as he started reading the details, rocking back and forth on his heels like a child.

"We got to go there. That's where we're going to see this thing."

Only by divine timing and intervention could two men, once worlds and opinions apart, be brought together in unison with an event, such as a rocket launch.

"Dad, I have never seen you this excited about anything in my life. I thought you had seen one before. I've been wanting to see one since I was a kid. It's been a dream of mine." I leaned back in my chair, holding its arms, and waited for his response.

"Michael, when I was thirteen years old, I wanted to see a rocket launch out into space. I was in college when we landed on the moon. I got to tell you that was unreal. Humans leaving Earth to land somewhere entirely new? Just the sheer thought of us landing on the moon away from this place is just mind-blowing."

"How come you haven't seen a launch? I thought it would be pretty easy to see those."

"C'mon man! It's one of the most intricate things you can possibly accomplish. The amount of things that have to go right for a launch to happen is almost godly. There are nine million parts that have to work properly on the rocket. The weather has to be perfect. Calculations have to be made without any margin for error. One degree, one decimal point off, and the whole thing goes to crap. I have been close twice in my lifetime, but they both got canceled at the last minute."

Dad stared down on his phone, smiling from ear to ear, reading more about the launch. Our dream—our shared, lifelong dream—was within a couple of days' grasp. He pulled the phone closer to me, showing me the countdown. "1 day, 23 hours, and 54 seconds." I looked at him and watched; though he saw the timer countdown, his face changed to a look of disbelief. It was as though a lifetime of fleeting moments culminated in the form of a news announcement, only for him to denounce the probability of it even happening. The smile on his face quickly shifted to a frown, then to the familiar look he had donned for years. It is a look of *never getting too high in the moment* when something spectacular happens for him. It is a look where no matter how good things are, expect the highs to turn to lows. Peaks and valleys, he calls them. I watched him stare in disbelief that he might finally see something he has wanted to see. It was heartbreaking to see the doubt. So I asked him about it.

"Dad, how come you're not excited about this anymore?"

He sat, wading through the information on his phone.

"Every time I have wanted to see a rocket launch, and even *been* in Florida to experience it, I was always disappointed. Something didn't work out. Weather, crew, any little thing would get it canceled. So I don't count on ever seeing one. Even as I'm reading this, I can't help but think it won't happen."

"Yeah, but Dad, we got to stay positive that we're going to see it. Cocoa Beach isn't that far away from us. We don't leave until Sunday. It's divine timing. We're supposed to see it."

"Yeah, well." Dad swayed from side to side. I sensed his dejection pushing him from right to left, the thirteen-year-old inside of him afraid of feeling let down once again. At seventy-four, there he was—close to something he had been waiting his whole life to see, but, of course, he could only control so much of achieving his own dream. He knew this; he understood the reality of his chances. I couldn't help but feel for him and understood his lack of hope.

"I mean, it's two days from now. A lot can happen." I tried to sound assuring. He kept reading more on his phone, not responding for a few moments. He drew a breath, a heavy exhale as he read further looking for an answer, any sign that things were going to work out in his favor to see the rocket launch. He digressed from his search, losing any optimism in it happening.

"Son, when you reach my age, there becomes a point where you get tired of trying to fit everything into your life. It's just not possible. And sometimes, you don't get to see what you want to see or experience what you want to happen. When you understand this, you realize that you don't *need* everything. You don't need a whole lot. You have what you have. You're blessed for having something—anything, for that matter. And you move on. I have been blessed with the chance to build my castle my entire life. I spent years building it. I have worked so dang hard for it. Now, I want to enjoy it. I haven't been able to until now. These are my golden years."

All I could think about was how devotedly my dad went to church for his whole life—as committed as a bodybuilder showing up to the gym daily. Maybe God could pull some strings for us. We could finally see our boyhood dreams come to life. There was a peace to it though, alongside what felt like a heartbreaking urgency. At that moment, my dad seemed content to never see a rocket launch. Maybe it wasn't in the cards for him in this lifetime. If he did, he did. If he didn't, then he didn't. He was good either way.

And there is something to be gained from such contentment and satisfaction. Our whole lives are determined by a single force: to stay busy, hustle, work harder, go faster, study more. What we have now is never enough. We always have to have more. And we miss out on what we have in our possession. We focus so much on the building of our castles that we miss out on the joy that we even have a castle to build. We wait until we are old in age to enjoy what we've built. Watching Dad immersed in his phone, standing in silence, made me realize that life is not about how much you acquire or how much you do. It is about how much you enjoy it. Just the fact that we had a chance to even share a hope of *possibly* seeing a launch was a worthy moment in itself. Obviously, it would be much cooler to see one, but even having the opportunity was more precious than I initially realized. And if it worked out, it would be the first time I'd get to experience something new with my dad that would be a first for us both.

He wouldn't get distracted like he often did when I was a kid, and it was his turn to pick me up from school. Most of my memories from then are of 5:00 p.m., of him motioning me to get in the car fast because he was on the phone talking to his business partners or clients. I learned very quickly that telling him what happened at school was of no interest to him; therefore, I kept my days to myself. Even when something cool happened at basketball practice or at recess playing touch football, he would motion for me to lower my voice, a sign to tell him later when he wasn't on the phone.

But now, he wasn't going to make excuses about taking phone calls in the middle of weekend camping trips or sports events. He was going to be standing next to me in Cocoa Beach, hopefully watching history with me. He was going to show up. To hit the pause button on building the final touches of his castle so we could put a memory in the box. It had to happen. I had to have this memory. It was too perfect, too good for it not to happen.

We're hours away from the launch. The weather still looks good. Both of us have the windows rolled down, and we're listening to the sound of the ocean wind passing us by on a warm November night. We've said very little to each other outside of putting words to our anticipation. The closer we get to Cocoa Beach, the bigger the smile on my dad's face grows. He exudes freedom as he drives alongside the Atlantic Ocean.

I pray as we get closer. I tell God I need this to happen. *Just give me this moment, please, one moment to have with him where I could remember this for the rest of my life.* I just want this thing to be a special moment burned into my brain—one to negate the years we didn't have together. The fighting, the yelling, the cursing of his name in the depths of a packed bowl of weed while sitting in my studio apartment at my mom's house. I lived those years with such anger and pain. I believe it could all go away with this launch. And I want it to. I also want my dad to experience the freedom from the years he spent working, building and building, and hardly stopping to enjoy what he had created. I pray harder, closing my eyes as I inhale the salt-laced air from the sea.

======

A mile from the beach, we stop at a 7-11 where I buy some peanut butter M&Ms and sparkling water. In the short distance from where we are is the Ron Jon Surf Shop: a world-famous establishment that's been around since the 1950s.

"Let's go in there," I tell him.

"Why do you want to go in there?" he says.

"It's Ron Jon. This place is famous. Let's go check it out."

We enter the shop, and I wind through all the board shorts and surfing t-shirts. I turn to look for Dad, and he's gone. My dad has a habit of exploring his environments on his own. It's in his nature to see and experience things for himself. He doesn't tell you that he's going to look at something that intrigues him. He just goes and looks. I have spent a quarter of my time on past trips looking for him.

Tonight, as I look for him, I realize that I am the same way too, venturing off into new environments and into new places, always filled with curiosity. This trait serves us well. For Dad, wandering off on his own looks like driving across the country, working in his garden, exploring historical American landmarks, and pondering the mechanics of the man and machine relationship. For me, wandering is exploring the world, venturing in and out of museums in Amsterdam and Belgium, and grazing food carts in Spain and Italy. It is writing and deep conversations about our whys, our existence, and our purposes. Venturing off on my own fuels an inherent freedom I received from him to see, hear, and be. At other times, wandering on my own creates a sense of isolation, a heightening feeling of discomfort of being on your own in a new place. My phone rings and his face pops up on the screen.

"Where are you?" he asks.

"I'm over near the Hawaiian shirts."

"Come over to the longboard section. They got some cool stuff here."

"Alright, I'll be right over."

I smile as I hang up the phone. A short distance from where I am, I see his black hat, the gray hairs sprouting from underneath. I slow my gait and watch him browse the store, staring into the high corners of their ceiling. He's probably thinking about how much time it took and how many men were needed to build this giant shop we are standing in. He squints when he concentrates. It makes me proud that I have inherited such curiosity from him. He ventures to an area where a group of men saw pieces of wood in the remodeled section of the store.

"You see anything you like, Dad?"

"Not really, I mean . . ." He pauses and turns his attention back to the men building a makeshift cabinet that looks like it will be used to hold more t-shirts. I go to one of the nearby t-shirt racks and see a style and fit that catches my eye. There is a t-shirt, long-sleeved and blue, hanging on a rack. I grab it and notice a picture of an old-school Woody with a surfboard on it and these words underneath: *It's All About the Ride.*

"What do you think of this?" I show him.

"I like it," he says. I tell him that I am going to the checkout line, and he puts his hand up in acknowledgment, turning his focus back on the cabinet project. The cashier greets me, and I place a couple of items on the counter, waiting to see if my dad would take me up on my offer. She scans the items, waiting with empty hands for whatever else I'll be purchasing. I tell her I'm waiting on my dad. She nods. He is rummaging through dark colors and shades of green and blue.

"Dad, are you getting anything?" I yell to him.

"Yeah, just a second." He continues to flip through racks of clothes and pulls out a shirt, shoving it underneath his arm. He approaches the counter and lays the shirt on top. It's the exact same one I chose.

"You got the same shirt as me?"

"Yeah, I thought it was cool. Now, you and I got something to share."

It was the first time on the trip, in fact in my life, that I could remember my dad expressing joy in sharing something with me. "It's All About the Ride" had very little to do with the back of the shirt. It was something he used to tell me as a kid. He never was one for the destination. For him, it was always about how you got there. This whole trip was about the ride too. As much as we both want to see a rocket, and as much fun as we had at the race, it will always be about him and me being together on this journey.

He smiles at me as I hand him his shirt on the way to the van. He puts it on over the shirt he is wearing.

"What do you think of it? Does it look good on me?" he asks, still grinning, pulling out the wrinkles.

"Yeah, it does. What do you think of my shirt? Does it look good on me?"

"I mean, it looks alright." He starts to laugh, flaunting his shirt in front of me. "I guess we'll see who wears it better." We both laugh, placing our bags in the backseat of the car as we buckle up to find better parking.

"Wait," he says. "Before we go, I have something else for us." My dad has a smaller bag sitting on his lap, fitting comfortably in the crevice between his two legs. He rummages through it and pulls out a rubber ducky with a beach ball and a Hawaiian shirt.

"Every voyage, every ship and crew, must have a mascot. This is ours."

He centers the duck on top of the dashboard, creating an even divide between the driver and passenger side of our sprinter van.

"I dub thee Commander Quack, mascot of Van Force One." I knight the duck in a poor English accent, and my dad laughs. For a second or two, we make eye contact, realizing this spectacular ride is almost over. We have spent the past eleven days sharing our pasts, coming to terms with our lost time with one another, and wishing deep down we could have it all back. We shared what most fathers and sons share with each other over many years—the passing of our generational traits and curses. These are the things that keep us up all night, that will haunt us for days to come.

These are also the things that make us who we are, shape and form us to be strong, to provide, and to take hold of our duties. In my lifetime, Dad never said a word about his anxieties, the curses that kept him up at night. He never said a word about the nights where he couldn't sleep when money coming into the business started to slow down. He never mentioned the heartbreaks of his past loves, the up and down ride of grieving and healing after his divorces. Before this trip, Dad never said anything about venturing off into monasteries to sit in silence, to find out after many years of broken patterns why he felt lost, confused, and questioned his existence. Until this trip, my dad was a mystery to me.

And I now know why. He never wanted me to worry about him. He wanted to do everything he could to keep my life on the straight and narrow, to make sure it was much easier for me than it was for him. He didn't let me in because it was all about him giving me something better than what he got: a future. I disliked him all these years because I never knew what he had sacrificed for me. And he never mentioned a word about it. For thirty-seven years, Dad never told me he was scared at times and he worried at times. He never told me until this trip that he was amazed when I came into this world as his son. He enjoyed watching me grow when he had me at the Eagle's Nest on Orange Ave. He was proud of me when—more than anything I had ever done—I came home from boot camp as a young, lean Marine ready for the Middle East.

The joy we now share in the van, placing Commander Quack at the helm of Van Force One, melts away years of self-induced fear that I might end up like Dad: misunderstood, overly complicated, utterly alone. He is, though, nothing like I thought he was. In fact, he's better than I ever thought he would be.

———

It is dark on the shores of Cocoa Beach. Groups of people are scattered throughout the area, and Dad and I await history to unfold before us. We find a spot close to the water, where the ocean spray hits the backs of my legs.

He stands next to me, his arms folded across his body with his feet spread a bit wider than his normal stance.

"This is going to be cool, huh, Dad?"

"Yeah, yeah . . . I mean it better be. We made it this far."

We did make it this far. We made it thousands of miles for a race and are leaving this short season as father and son.

A blast of orange flames starts to grow beneath the rocket at Cape Canaveral, and in a matter of minutes, we watch as it blasts into orbit, disappearing from our vision. It is everything we had hoped for. Neither of us ever thought we would see a rocket launch into orbit— one with people on it, no less.

Dad had seen the moon landing, and now he's seen a live launch. There is no money, no price, nothing in the world that could ever take away the memory of watching him watch this—with the excitement and wonderment of a thirteen-year-old from New Jersey, having waited his whole life for the one day he could watch a rocket blast into space. It is the memory, the story, I have always wanted to share with him.

And there we stand, long after the rocket blinks out of sight, the two of us experiencing our childhood dreams coming true—together.

GO SEE YOUR PARENTS

On the morning of our last day, I plug in and charge all of my electronics on my side of the hotel room. Camera, Zoom recorder, phone, Apple watch . . . all dangling from the wall like vines from a tree.

"Jeez, Michael. You bring enough gear with you?" he smirks.

"Can't help it, Dad. The Marine in me is used to carrying a bunch of gear. Got to be prepared, right?"

He starts to laugh in disbelief.

"You know," I say, starting to pack all my gear and dirty clothes away into a bag, "I brought all this stuff with me because I wanted to document this trip. I wanted to create a memory for both of us and write it all down. Believe it or not, Dad, this has been one of the coolest trips I've ever been on in my life. We got to drive cross-country—hit the road and see America. You told me some great stories. I shared some with you. We laughed. We got to see a rocket launch together. How cool is that?"

He stands behind the other queen bed, notebook in hand.

"And I'm really glad you invited me, Dad. Thank you."

He pauses for a moment, the notebook starting to quiver in his hand, just like his breath as he starts to tell me something I never thought in a million years I would hear from him.

"Son, when you write this book, please tell people to go see their parents. Go get in an RV, a car, anything, and just tell them to drive somewhere with them. Tell them they don't need to know where they are going. Just go get them and bring them on the road. Because you're getting to the age where most people lose their parents and . . ."

There have been two times in my life I have seen Dad cry the way he does right now in the hotel room. The other time was when I was twelve years old in Healdsburg, underneath the midnight-black sky. Our house didn't have street lights. There wasn't a street light around for quite a distance. Every weekend that I spent with him up in the country house—as we called it—Dad would walk me out to the front gate to make sure it was locked and we would look at the stars above. The stars were so bright, so luminous. You didn't need any light other than theirs and the moon's. My dad always harped on how I'd still bring a flashlight to lock the gate.

"Use your night vision," he used to say.

Dad always admired the stars, but this night was different. After we locked the gate, he turned me around by the shoulder.

"Look up, son."

The stars were exceptionally bright that night. We could see the planets, satellites flying overhead. Blinking lights from late-night flights slowly gliding across the sky. Shooting stars that disappeared in a blink of an eye.

"Isn't that something? How big God is."

I didn't know what to say to him then, as I was still grappling with being in Catholic school and wondering how it was possible to believe in something I could not see. And there was Dad, telling me that God was so big, so vast—everywhere—that we just couldn't fathom it. He held my hand tighter and in the darkness, my night vision made out tears of release and love. It was just him and me out there together. We stood in silence. We looked up and we never said anything to each other. I just let him cry.

Standing in that room with him now, he starts to cry those same tears. I go over to him and grab his hand and hold him like he held me when I was twelve.

"Dad, I love you."

"I love you too, son. Thanks for coming with me on this trip. I had an awesome time. I am really happy we did this."

As I hold him, I can't let go of the idea that he will not be here someday, and that him being here in my arms right now is a gift. Every minute counts. And I hug him tighter to let him know I love him no matter how much I used to hate him. All those times I was mad at him are gone. All the memories of him running late and making me feel like nothing, the nights he would cancel our plans, the sheer scorn of feeling unloved—they are gone. Nothing but this moment matters.

In eleven days and across 2000-plus miles, I have forgiven myself and my dad for a lifetime of regret. I finally know what he meant when he said God was so big and so vast that we could not understand Him.

Out of all the birthday gifts I could have received in this world, God gave me the best gift of all. He gave me a hug from my dad who held me as I held him.

———

On the flight from Florida, he asks me if I would want to go to Sebring with him again next year for the race. I immediately say yes. He smiles as I tell him I am all in. The plane makes a connecting stop in Denver, and we deboard the plane. He has to catch a connecting flight back home to California, and I have to catch an Uber back to my apartment.

As we slowly make our way off the plane, he looks at me and smiles while holding his signature black notebook. He looks good for seventy-four. "Healthy as an ox," he describes himself. He takes pride that his doctor can't believe he's not on any sort of medication. He still rubs it in my face the fact that he can do more pull-ups than me. I tend to agree. He tells me that he's looking forward to March and traveling with me again. I smile and look forward to it too.

He has to rush to his flight when he realizes everyone else is beginning to board. I had hoped for a hug, another moment to hold him as long as possible. Time only allows for a fist bump and an unspoken peace between us. No longer are we enemies. We are no longer cordial for the sake of the family. We are friends; we are family; we are father and son.

"I love you, son. Get home safe," he says as he rolls his suitcase and in an expedited manner, moves toward his gate.

———

I used to be able to say no to my dad. I can't anymore. I say yes now. When he calls, I pick up. When he texts me, I shoot him a note back. When he invites me on another road trip, I'll do it. Even if it means I have to work more and sleep less, I will say yes to more memories that I will carry with me for the rest of my life. It is an honor to live his golden years with him.

THE ROAD AHEAD AND MILES BEHIND

In March of 2021, Dad and I went back to Sebring to pick up Van Force One. We had left it there as planned, hoping to be lucky enough to go see the race again since it had been rescheduled because of COVID. We slept close to the same campground as last time. We ate good food and we got to watch the race at the start of a humid, Florida spring. On the drive back, we barely stopped, and we talked a whole lot.

Today, Dad and I talk almost every day. We talk about the same things we always have—sports, business, and money—but every once in a while, Dad brings up the trip with me. He'll ask me how life is on my end. I can hear him smiling through the phone when he does. It's the gift I have always wanted. To have him and I talk like friends, like men, like father and son. We're planning more trips in the future.

He'll be seventy-five this year, and he's full of energy. He's even gone on some trips with my brothers, and it has been incredible to see them get time to create memories with him of their own on those road trips.

My moments with Dad count more with each passing day. It inspires me to take more risks in my life. To do everything I can to make things worthwhile. There is more adventure in my life because of what Dad shared about getting on the bus and figuring it out, no matter the circumstance. When doors are closed to opportunities and connections, I now keep my heart open as much as possible to keep myself in the fight, to tell myself that God will take care of the rest if I let Him in my life, just like I let Dad in on our trip. The more I say yes, the more things happen for me.

I said yes to this story. I said yes to the crying and to the laughter that came with it. I said yes to acknowledging and accepting that I am my father's son. Dad and I are more alike than we are the same. And I love that about him. I love that about me. And that is the road we're headed on. Exploring how the two of us, after miles and miles, can create new memories, new experiences, and put all the other stuff behind us for the sake of something new and bountiful.

In life, you will always have the road ahead of you and the miles behind. It will come to an end one day. For now, there is a bunch of highways ahead of you. They're vast and open. They can be straight, or they can be full of twists and turns. You have to keep your eyes on them. Sure, it's good to reflect on the miles and the distance you've come. But don't get caught up in the rearview mirror looking back at everything, particularly the negative stuff. Don't do that with yourself, and especially, don't do it with your parents. It's never too late to create something new with them. I thought it was way too late for Dad and me to have anything at all. That road trip saved us. The road taught us that we can coexist. We can be different and be the same. We can love each other. My hope is that what you read will help you see your parents differently, like how I got to see my Dad. For Dad and I, we look back at the miles we put on in our relationship and on the trip with contentment. We look forward to the road ahead. A different path.

He and I have started new and fresh. As men. As friends. As father and son.

NOTES FROM THE ROAD

Thank you for reading this book. It means the world to me. I hope you enjoyed it as much as I loved writing it. Below are small tidbits and thoughts I recorded from the road trip that I want to share with you. These stood out to me the most:

There is something particularly spiritual about a road trip, I've found. Riding a long way in a car can, in a way, help you solve your most complex problems as you inevitably confront and explore the deepest parts of yourself. The hidden parts you have always wondered about. Where you go is not as important as how you get there. You'll find the answers along the journey. I believe road trips are the purest form of self-discovery. Seek and you will find.

 —My journal entry from Day 1

Never forget that your parents always want to be a part of your life. Even if you don't need them they still need you.
 —Dad

If this is what you want, get on the bus. If it's working, you'll adjust. If it's not working, you'll adjust. Just get on the bus.
 —Dad

You'll stop worrying about things and wanting them when you realize you can't understand God and the universe.
 —Dad

Tell your body you love it when it hurts. Give it positive energy, and it will respond.
 —Dad

A man with a plan always wins.
 —Dad and/or General George Patton

After a while, you stop chasing things. You become happy with what you have. Do you want to spend your whole life building something you can't enjoy? Build your castle and then enjoy it.
 —Dad

I have a request. If you or anyone you know is planning a road trip with their parents, please share your story with me on Instagram @mike.liguori.

Get your free guide to lessons and more
from the road trip at
http://mikeliguori.com/roadahead

ABOUT THE AUTHOR

Mike Liguori is the CEO of Live Your Truth Media, a content production company that helps brands and companies utilize the power of podcasting to build deeply connected audiences. He has worked with some amazing companies, such as *Huffington Post*, T Mobile, and Toyota. In addition to this work, Mike published the memoir, *The Sandbox: Stories of Human Spirit and War*. His story of military service and reflections have been featured in the *Huffington Post*, *Thrive Global*, *San Jose Mercury News*, among other places. He lives in Scottsdale, Arizona.

A free ebook edition is available with the purchase of this book.

To claim your free ebook edition:

1. Visit MorganJamesBOGO.com
2. Sign your name CLEARLY in the space
3. Complete the form and submit a photo of the entire copyright page
4. You or your friend can download the ebook to your preferred device

Print & Digital Together Forever.

Snap a photo

Free ebook

Read anywhere